I WAS CHAPLAIN ON THE *FRANKLIN*

I Was Chaplain

on the

Franklin

FATHER JOSEPH T. O'CALLAHAN, S.J.

Naval Institute Press

Annapolis, Maryland

Naval Institute Press
291 Wood Road
Annapolis, MD 21402

First Naval Institute Press paperback edition published in 2019.
   ISBN: 978-1-68247-477-8 (paperback)
   ISBN: 978-1-68247-478-5 (eBook)

The Library of Congress has cataloged the hardcover edition as follows:
Library of Congress catalog card number: 56—10786

⊗ Print editions meet the requirements of ANSI/NISO z39.48–1992 (Permanence
of Paper).
Printed in the United States of America.

23 22 21 20   5 4 3

Contents

CHAPTER ONE

A Chaplain Reports Aboard

IT WAS January, 1945. I was well out of range of the shooting on a cushion assignment at Ford Island, the pearl of Pearl Harbor. I was expecting a new assignment—staff duty, I hoped, in the Philippines. My sister Alice, a Maryknoll nun (her name in religion is Sister Rose Marie), had been imprisoned there since early in the war when the Japs had captured Manila. For three years neither my mother nor myself had heard a word of her. We did not know whether she was alive or dead.

The battle of Manila was at its height. Daily the headlines shouted of wholesale murder: "Japs in defeat go berserk." Even if "La" had survived the early phases of the war, such news gave us little hope that she still lived. Were I assigned to the Philippines, I could make inquiries and perhaps settle my mother's uncertainty which was in its way more taxing than even the worst, but definite, news would have been.

Throughout the first two months of 1945 I waited, performing the usual round of duties assigned to a chaplain in the vast "playing at house" that is the shorebound Navy. I listened to gripes, shuttled between the men and their officers on many small and some important missions of reconciliation. I arranged movies, coffee breaks, and fulfilled all the apparently picayune roles given to that mother-psychologist-efficiency expert, the unmilitary morale officer. At the same time I said Mass, heard confessions, and tried in an inadequate way to stretch the scope of my intentions and ministrations to the size of the need of a world at war. But mostly I waited.

On March 2nd I received from Captain John Moore, the fleet chaplain for Admiral Nimitz, unofficial word. The Philippines were out. My dispatch orders were coming through and they were not what I had hoped.

Two hours later the orders arrived:

To Joseph T. O'Callahan, 087280, Lieutenant Commander, USNR: Hereby detached from Chaplain duties, Naval Air Station, Pearl Harbor. Proceed immediately and without delay, reporting for duty to Commanding Officer, USS *Franklin* (CV-13).

Unlike most Navy orders, these dispatch orders meant exactly what they said. Navy terminology has acquired through the years an almost legal precision, often quite at variance with the ordinary meaning of words. "Proceed" means "Go within four days exclusive of travel time." "Proceed immediately" shrinks your packing period to forty-eight hours. But when to this the phrase "without delay" is added, one reports the same day that orders are received.

A chaplain was wanted for a carrier about to sail into the battle zone—a chaplain familiar with flattops and not new to combat. Combat orders are always welcome, but to me in 1945 they were decidedly a second choice. Word of my sister must wait.

In yet another sense, the *Franklin* was a second choice. The USS *Ranger* was my first ship.

To whatever ship one is assigned, whether it be carrier

or cruiser, dreadnought or destroyer, loyalty is due and peculiar affection is expected. Each ship derives a personality, an individuality, which is a distillation of the best traits of the individual persons who compose her crew. Any Navy ship has the right to expect that those assigned to duty with her will contribute something to her spirit and give her both their loyalty and their affection.

Sea duty to any naval man is naturally preferable to shore duty and, to one who has been connected with naval aviation, aircraft carriers are superior to any other ship. They are the queens of the fleet, Fighting Ladies, always in the thick of the fray.

But no ship, not even the queens of the fleet, would expect loyalty to such an extreme as to demand that any member of her crew forget that "First ship is first love." The *Ranger* had been my first ship. She always will be my first love. In this there is no difference between me and any other Navy man.

From the day I entered the Navy, I sought sea duty and I wanted to be aboard a carrier. I had had duty aboard a carrier; that carrier was the *Ranger*.

I had waited long for her. My first tour of duty was at the Naval Air Station, Pensacola. In my eighteen months there I had learned naval procedure and acquired an amateur familiarity with naval aviation. I had made hosts of friends: administrative heads who were now captains and executives of carriers; aviation instructors who now in war were the squadron leaders of planes flying from flattops into combat; many hundreds of cadets who had earned their wings at Pensacola and were now piloting those combat planes from carriers; other hundreds of mechanics and metalsmiths and radiomen, the bluejackets and chiefs who kept those carrier planes in good flying condition.

After Pearl Harbor Day most of my Pensacola Navy friends had gone to war in carriers. Eventually and happily, my orders to the *Ranger* had enabled me to join some of them. Although Pensacola had taught me naval procedure and naval aviation, my whole life prior to reporting aboard the *Ranger* had been entirely innocent of ships, and in this case at least, innocence was ignorance.

"Go aboard, face forward thus; on your right is starboard; the other side is port." With such seriocomic instructions, the Pensacola Navy had indoctrinated me into seaboard life. I admit this rule is easy to remember, but I found it not easy of application. When reporting aboard the *Ranger* I found myself on a hangar deck so big and symmetrical I could not tell where was forward and where aft.

I trust that the *Ranger* crew found me a ready pupil. I found them willing and expert instructors, particularly Scotty, the electrician, and Vermersch, the carpenter, and young Peterson, the gunner who bled to death in his bomber as she returned from a strike at Casablanca.

As I have said, a ship acquires a spirit which is a sort of Gestalt, a whole greater than the best traits of her entire complement. The spirit of the *Ranger* was superb. From the ranks, through the warrant and junior officers, to Andy the air officer, Johnny Hoskins the executive, and Captain Cal Durgin, the skipper—from all these the *Ranger* derived her greatness.

Seldom did the *Ranger* make headlines, and her praises are not sung in Navy folklore, as is the case with other carriers. However dangerous her war duty, it was not as consistently spectacular as were the assignments of other ships. But she didn't need headlines to be a great ship. She sailed the Atlantic from the arctic to the equator. Aboard her we dodged torpedoes and took part in the invasion of

North Africa, and we worried with her after hit-and-run raids against the Germans in Norway.

Now the *Ranger* has long since been decommissioned and sold for scrap, and the public does not know about the lonesome vacuum in the hearts of those who were her crew. Yet in a sense the *Ranger* participated in the glories of the newer carriers. I believe that every first-line carrier built during the war received a large complement of *Ranger*-trained men. If the new ships had the old carrier spirit, this was derived at least in part from her simple greatness.

Aboard the *Ranger* I spent two and one half years of war. Except for short periods of shipyard overhaul, we were constantly in combat waters. I think the best work of my Navy career was performed aboard her. And if no one knows about it except the men of the *Ranger* themselves, that is as it should be. By an accident of publicity my work aboard the *Franklin* is well known, but the credit for that work has a twofold source: priestly credit is due to my long years of Jesuit training; Navy credit is due to my carrier life aboard the *Ranger* under the direction of Johnny Hoskins and Cal Durgin.

Even with my unofficial advance notice, my dispatch orders to the *Franklin* did not allow much time to pack a cruise box, or say farewell to friends. Most of the time was used in going through the cumbersome process of formal detachment from my current assignment at the air station. Farewells had to be omitted, and not a few friends scarcely had learned that I had gone before they heard I had returned.

I said personal farewell and paid official respects to Captain Peterson, the Commanding Officer at Ford Island. I found time to telephone the district chaplain, Father Maurice Sheehy, to say goodbye and to ask a favor. In his position he would hear about those who were rescued from Jap prisons. He might hear about my sister, and might be able to help her if she were alive. Then I packed my bag and sea chest and went to Fox Two.

Wartime security forbade publication of maps revealing locations of the many piers and docks at Pearl Harbor. The enemy would never be able to decipher the peculiar designation by which any single dock was known, and yet its identity was not hidden under a subtle nomenclature thought out by experts of counterespionage. Only routine Navy habit was responsible for names familiar to all the Navy, yet mysterious to anyone else. The word "Ford" begins with the letter F, and the Navy signal word for F is "Fox." With peculiar logic, therefore, the docks at Ford Island were always called "Fox Docks." Never once did I hear any mention of a Ford Island dock. "Fox Two" was concise and clear to all familiar with Navy jargon.

It was not visiting day at Fox Two; it was a longshoreman's nightmare! Crates were piled high, boldly marked "CV13," the code letters for the *Franklin*. Onto the pier trucks unloaded canisters of shells, ammunition for the twenty-millimeter and forty-millimeter antiaircraft guns. An ammunition dump of small-caliber shells was rising on the dock. Planes, usually so graceful in the air, their normal medium, now lurched and jerked awkwardly in that same medium at the end of the ship's crane. They were in the air but not of it, tethered, pinned, and writhing with indignity. The planes had priority on the crane, and hundreds of sacks of potatoes, of cabbage, sugar, and flour had to be carried aboard by hand.

Two gangways joined pier to ship. Across one, an endless chain of men hauled provisions. On the other a similar gang loaded ammunition. Trying not to disturb the rhythm of the boys carrying their heavy loads, I slipped into line at the forward gangway and officially reported aboard the *Franklin* between two bags of potatoes.

"Permission to come aboard, sir, reporting for duty." Even amid the bedlam of last-minute preparations for sea, Navy courtesies are not forgotten. The officer of the day, on duty on the quarter-deck, smartly answered my salute.

The quarter-deck, as everyone knows who has ever read even a single story of the sea, is a very official, formal, almost sacred part of the ship. Yet, not everyone knows that in a carrier the quarter-deck is segregated from the mundane section of the vast hangar space by a merely imaginary line. Shift the imaginary line, and the quarter-deck likewise shifts. On a carrier the quarter-deck is not a deck; it is not even a place. It is merely a relation, an entity difficult to define philosophically, as all thinkers have found. The quarter-deck is wherever the officer of the deck says it is. And let no dog bark!

When I reported aboard the *Franklin*, the imaginary line which guards the quarter-deck's solemn precincts was seriously threatened. The mountains of potatoes and flour and cabbage, and the dumps of small-caliber ammunition, were rapidly disappearing from the dock. With equal rapidity new mountains and new dumps appeared on the hangar deck, threatening to engulf the quarter-deck. But the invisible line was invincible; the intangible majesty of the quarter-deck was inviolate. Despite the bedlam, here was order and authority. Within it the timeless rubrics of the sea prevailed.

"Permission granted," and that moment was officially recorded in the ship's log by the officer of the deck: "1535 Chaplain O'Callahan reports for duty."

I delayed a detailed check-in to the various departments

of the ship until such time as the senior officers were less hectically busy. After a brief courtesy call on Joe Taylor, the executive, I was free to look around.

On a carrier the hangar deck is the main deck; the deck below is the second deck; and successively farther down are the third and fourth. The number of each deck above the hangar level is prefixed by a zero. From 01 a sailor climbs to 02 and, continuing, ascends in the island structure until he reaches decks 08 and 09. Name plates at all hatches accurately designate both deck level and compartment number.

But in practice most decks have their own special names. I have never heard anyone refer to the fo'c'sle as the 01 deck. The 02 deck is known universally as the gallery deck. It would sound silly to talk about the 03 deck when you meant the flight deck. Which all seems to prove that whatever the mathematical niceness of a logical system of nomenclature, our everyday common-sense speech, though less logical, is more practical.

The hangar deck not only is the main deck of a carrier; it is also the best vantage point from which to appraise the size of this class of vessel. The hangar extends almost the entire length of the ship, with no obstructing bulkhead athwart. It is an enclosed space as big as three football fields. It is a floating airplane garage where planes are stored and repaired. Three gigantic elevators lift planes from hangar to flight deck in ten seconds. The platform of the elevator, when flush in the *up* position, actually comprises a section of the take-off area.

During flight operations the hangar deck is an important, noisy, and dangerous place. Important, because airplanes are the important weapons of a carrier; noisy, because the enclosing sides of the ship confine and magnify the roar of many engines; dangerous, because many propellers are revolving in a confined space.

As I made my first inspection of the *Franklin,* the hangar deck was noisy, not with the roar of engines, but with the bustle of some four hundred men engaged in storing provisions. All this activity was important because food and ammunition are important to a fighting ship. The hangar was dangerous, but the danger lacked the dignity of combat. Danger lurked in a canister of shells heaved onto the pile— not danger of being blown up, but of being bowled over. Danger lay in a potato rolled from a defective bag or a dropped banana. Sliding on a banana is traditionally the quintessence of indignity, but extremely perilous to ankle and spine. Ask the man who's done it!

The heaps of provisions and the stacks of ammunition never quite succeeded in smothering the hangar space reserved for planes. Almost as fast as the stuff came aboard, it was stored below deck in proper compartments, each readily accessible at sea and yet all carefully segregated.

A housekeeper with a very small apartment, with limited refrigerator bins and closets, will properly appreciate this storage problem. Heavily laden with bundles, she has returned from the supermarket. Now where can she store these scores of items, at the moment overflowing the kitchen table?

The supply officer of a carrier has a housekeeper's headache many times intensified. He must keep food on hand for ten thousand meals each day. When he gets a new shipment of supplies, he must get enough to last for eight weeks. And his supermarket—the general Navy Warehouse—makes its deliveries at the last possible moment. The supply officer has the job of systematically storing these overwhelming quantities of provisions below deck, and must have everything shipshape before putting to sea.

Shortly before sailing time the after section of the hangar deck looks like a warehouse for heavy industry. Here are scores of extra airplane engines, extra wings, and crates of airplane parts in sufficient quantity and diversity to construct many new airplanes and to guarantee proper repair of planes in the forward area no matter what the combat or operational damage. All this gear must be stored below deck before the ship puts to sea. But first each item must be carefully catalogued so that when needed it can be found with a minimum of delay.

The supply officer has the responsibility, but the actual manual work is done by the enlisted men. Three thousand men had dreamed or hoped for a holiday at Waikiki on the day before our departure for the war zone, but now they are not vacationers; they are longshoremen. They like neither the prospect nor the work. But they do it. When you come to know these boys well, you can tell just by watching the way they carry their sacks of flour whether they are plain disgusted or morosely mean. Happily, their complaints are healthy American gripes, not snarls.

Many people forget that besides actual combat there is much tough, distasteful work aboard ship. Such work is done by these boys. If they were not in the service for $90 a month, they would avoid the danger of war; and then, for these incidental, disagreeable tasks, they would be paid as much as $90 a week.

Happily for human contentment, distant inequalities make less impression on the mind than small present equalities. In the line of men loading provisions, no one works harder than anyone else. None of the crew would lounge on the beach at Waikiki until the ship had been entirely provisioned and all ammunition stored. Then, afterward, there might be time for a quick swim.

Along the *Franklin's* port side activity is specialized. The fuel barge is casting off lines. For two hours she has been alongside, pumping thousands of gallons of oil into the fuel tanks of the *Franklin*. The red flag of danger flies from her mast and flies as well from the yardarm of our ship.

At intervals the impersonal strident voice of the loudspeaker blared its message above the din of the hangar deck: "The smoking lamp is out while taking fuel—the smoking lamp is out throughout the ship."

Now the gasoline barge edges in, taking the position just vacated by the oiler. Lines secured, the pumps start and the peculiar odor of high-octane gas hovers in the air.

More frequently, more stridently, and more emphatically the loudspeaker blares its command: "The smoking lamp is out throughout the ship while pumping gasoline—the smoking lamp is out throughout the ship."

I have never seen a smoking lamp, and doubt that one has been lighted for many generations, perhaps not since the invention of "sulphur sticks." But the continued use of the sentence, "The smoking lamp is out," is one of the many links which connect a modern carrier with the old sailing days and ships of the line. In early times, when the smoking lamp was out, no flame was available from which the old tar might light his pipe. In heavy storms, when little wooden ships tossed on the waves, their smoking lamps were extinguished for safety. Now, aboard a much more dangerous type of warship, at times when a flame or a lighted cigarette would be especially dangerous, "the smoking lamp is out." Until the smoking lamp is relit, no one is allowed to smoke.

Lighting of the lamp is just as magical as the existence

of the quarter-deck. There is no visible lamp, no physical flame. The lamp is both created and lit by the official pronunciamento of the officer of the deck.

Not only is a modern carrier more dangerous than any ship of Farragut's fleet, or Dewey's or Sims'; it is also much more complicated. It is an airfield, a fortress, and a city. It is a city where more than three thousand men live and work. They work at as many diversified occupations as would be found in any industrial city and they live in such confined space that by comparison the most crowded tenement would seem spacious.

The living quarters for the crew are located for the most part on the second deck, that is, one deck below the hangar deck. To each man are allotted a locker and a bunk. The bunks are arranged in triple, sometimes in quadruple, tiers. The lowest is a few inches above the deck, the highest just below the overhead with space for a thin man to squeeze in.

Very narrow aisles separate the rows of bunks. To destroy the last vestige of privacy, the narrow aisle between these rows of bunks is the main passageway fore and aft on the second deck. An enlisted man aboard a warship has less privacy than any other known human being.

Junior officers fare somewhat better. The aisles in their bunk rooms are not primarily passageways. With added seniority, the officer finds that his bunk room contracts—it becomes a bedroom for four. Added rank warrants assignment to half a double bedroom. A few senior officers have small single rooms.

Fortunately, for the most part increase in rank and in age run apace. So the oldster, who would find complete absence of privacy an irritating burden, usually enjoys the privilege of a private room.

Youngsters do not seem to mind communal life. For the most part they enjoy the camaraderie of the bunk room.

Fastidiousness of table service is of even less concern to the boys. One dear lady, trying to offer constructive criticism to the Navy, suggested it would help morale if at mealtime white linen cloths adorned the mess tables. During seven years in the Navy I met thousands of boys, listened to tens of thousands of gripes and groans, complaints of major or minor import, sometimes warranted, sometimes unwarranted. Their suggestions ran the gamut of youthful ingenuity. But I never met a lad who had noticed that the mess tables were unclothed.

But the same boys were keenly aware of the dishes that went on the mess table. They wanted lots of food of good quality and adequate variety.

On the *Franklin,* messing compartments are located on the third deck. The mess kitchens cook ten thousand meals per day. They cook only for enlisted men.

Regulations do not allow the officers to obtain their meals from these kitchens. Officers have the facilities of the wardroom kitchen. When a ship is in port, or returns to port, the officers frequently can buy for their wardroom whatever delicacies might please their palate and their pocketbook. (When the ship is at sea for long periods, however, food for both officers and men comes from the same ship's stores.) The wardroom can buy the raw supplies, but the officers are denied the facilities of the ship's kitchens and the skill of the ship's cooks.

A chaplain, however, has peculiar indirect privileges, especially in the kitchen. In the *Ranger* it had been my practice to take one meal each day at the enlisted mess. I renewed this practice on my first day aboard the *Franklin.*

The source of this special permission was the commissary

officer. The reason he willingly granted it: the evident endorsement of his products by the chaplain. When the boys saw the chaplain eating in their mess by choice, any complaints they might have intended to make to him about the food would probably be dropped. As I got to know the lads better, they jokingly complained to me, not so much about the food as about myself. They charged that it couldn't be merely an accident that my daily sharing of their mess, whether breakfast, dinner, or supper, always occurred at the best meal of that particular day.

But they never had adequate evidence to prove the charge, because they never had opportunity to see me in the executive officer's room each Saturday night. On that night the menu for all the meals of the subsequent week was submitted for his approval. At the same time I gave my unofficial approval.

Adjacent to the mess kitchens are the bakeshops, the envy of any community. From these ovens every morning came hundreds of loaves of bread, good Navy bread. Unfortunately for the contentment of America, the art of creating homemade bread has been forgotten by the civilian world. But the Navy baker has retained the skill.

At the bakeshop my tour of the ship became less impersonal. Hitherto I had been a silent observer; now I became an active participant. One of the bakers invited me to test the bread. It seemed a good place to end my inspection of the *Franklin,* and better than most. I settled down with a hot cup of coffee and a fistful of fresh-baked Navy bread to express long-windedly my approval. It's always good to make friends with the baker.

CHAPTER TWO

Westward to War

THE VAST composition of men and ships that made up Task Force 58 had an important and dangerous function to fulfill. The Japanese naval force which had survived the crushing defeat of the Battle of the Philippine Sea had crept off, a tattered remnant, and left command of the Pacific to the Allied navies unchallenged. But, while these survivors might only constitute a pitiful fraction of the once-proud Imperial Navy, we knew they were a force to be reckoned with still—at least a force which could increase the estimated losses during the imminent invasion of Okinawa, unless they were removed from the scene. The cold logic of strategy made imperative that we search them out in their home waters and destroy them. A very hazardous task, and the task of Task Force 58.

And so, shortly after sunrise on the 3rd of March, 1945, the *Franklin* set sail from Pearl Harbor and headed for combat. About one half-hour before scheduled departure the order had been passed over the loudspeaker: "Man all special sea details!" About one-half of the ship's deck crew took their preassigned positions at the mooring lines. Each group of men is under the charge of an officer. By his side stands the "talker," a seaman wearing the headpiece of a sound-power phone. As the name indicates, sound is their power source. The energy of the spoken word generates the electricity which sends the message to all phones on the circuit. Use of the phones is a safety precaution. They ensure communication even in the unlikely event that the ship's regular electric power should fail.

For a short time Chaplain Gatlin and I watched activities on the fantail. This was the first time that Gats was really going to sea. On his trip from the States to Hawaii he had merely been a passenger. Now we were both part of this ship, and enjoying privileges which are not extended to passengers. We had the freedom of the ship with restrictions imposed only by common sense. We were careful not to interfere with those at work.

Our visit to the fantail was brief. The vantage place to watch a ship get under way is the fo'c'sle. Of course, the captain's bridge is headquarters for all sea operations at all times. Final decisions and orders come from there. But under the captain the first lieutenant is responsible for mooring and up-anchoring and similar functions of seamanship. His official station at such times is the fo'c'sle. Gats and I went to the fo'c'sle and watched Lieutenant Commander Robert Downes direct operations. He gave orders to his talker, who spoke the messages into the phone and reported acknowledgment from twenty-odd stations. Most commands were given in a low voice unheard by spectators even a short distance away. But suddenly we heard a short reprimand: "Bowen, pass the order exactly as I give it. Let me do the thinking. You just talk, but talk the words I say."

How often had I heard just that complaint about talkers! On every ship there seems to be the same difficulty. The talker thinks he is giving the message as he heard it, but he uses a few words of his own choice. At the next relay the newly worded message is again paraphrased, and soon the message, originally precise and clear, is garbled beyond recognition. On one occasion we ran a test aboard the *Ranger*. Unknown to the talkers, a wire recorder was put into a circuit of twelve phones. A series of technical orders was given to the first talker. The original words were then recorded—along with the subsequent distortions. In one case the word received at the twelfth station was a direct contradiction of the original message. When the talkers were later summoned to the library to hear the record of their voices, one lad suspected a trick. With supreme illogic he accepted the recorded voice as his own but insisted that he was not guilty of the distortion of the message! Only with such tests were the boys convinced that alert attention was needed for precise relay.

"Bowen, pass the word exactly as I give it," Robert Downes barked at his talker. I turned to Chaplain Gatlin: "Young Bowen might be down to see us before the day is through. I bet he doesn't even realize that he has used different words." This little incident of the phone talker is an illustration of a theory I have about chaplain duties. It is my opinion that much of his work is done out of his office, on tours of the ship. Chaplain Gatlin and myself were not merely spectators on the fo'c'sle; we were special observers. We were observing not merely the mechanics of getting a ship away from the docks; we were especially observing the reactions of these men who were our new parishioners. You get to know your parishioners better at their work than in your office. Do this, and when they come to the office the chaplain can understand them better for having seen them about the ship. He has had a chance to make proper judgments, to know whether to sympathize or correct. There is less danger of giving too much credence to one side of a story, less chance of bringing a boy's plea to official ears when the boy has no cause for resentment. On the other hand, if I appreciate the predicament of the first lieutenant and he knows it, then in some other case where a boy is entirely right, Robert Downes is more open to conviction. I don't think that a chaplain does his best work, feet cocked all day on his office desk.

But he should, of course, be available many hours each day in his office. So when the *Franklin* slipped through the narrows and the open submarine net, approached and passed abeam of Diamond Head, and the order sounded over the speaker, "Secure all special sea details," when we were really in the open sea, Gats and I went to our office in the ship's library.

The library is situated well aft on the second deck, starboard side. There is a hatch immediately to the rear connecting directly with the hangar deck. But at the moment some airplane engines were being tested in the hangar. It's always safer to avoid them. Besides, it's profitable to be familiar with several passageways between any two points in a ship. If one passage becomes blocked by an explosion in combat, knowledge of an alternate passage is useful. So Gats and I proceeded from the fo'c'sle by way of the Marine berthing compartments.

Chaplain business was slow. The ship's complement had only been aboard a few days, and the minor monastic tensions of shipboard life had not begun to develop. This was the time to make a study of the men and officers.

Chaplains have more official dealings with the executive officer than with anyone else aboard. Commander Joe Taylor was our "exec." Regular Navy, Annapolis 1927, he had won his wings at Pensacola in 1929. He had seen duty with patrol squadrons and with fighter squadrons, both aboard the old carrier *Langley* and, later, on the *Lexington*. In May, 1941, he assumed command of Torpedo Squadron 5, based on the aircraft carrier *Yorktown*. Shortly after the Pearl Harbor attack, he led his squadron in the raids on the Gilbert and Marshall Islands in February, 1942. Later he participated in the raids on Salamaua and Lae and then on Tulagi. He took part in the Battle of the Coral Sea in May, the first major engagement in naval history in which surface ships did not exchange a single shot; and, of more practical value, a battle in which the Japanese advance southward was checked. He flew in the Battle of Midway where the Japanese Navy suffered its first decisive defeat in 350 years, the battle which ended the Japanese offensive and somewhat restored the balance of naval power in the Pacific. For his services in command of Torpedo Squadron 5, based on the *Yorktown* until that carrier was lost in the Battle of Midway, June, 1942, he was awarded a Navy Cross and a Gold Star in lieu of a second Navy Cross.

The citations which accompanied these honors indicate that Joe Taylor is a brave fighting man. Navy Cross:

For extraordinary heroism and meritorious conduct as Commander of a Torpedo Squadron in a carrier air group in action against enemy Japanese forces at Tulagi Harbor and in the Coral Sea during the period of May 4–8, 1942. Due to Lieutenant Commander Taylor's distinguished and capable leadership, the high combat efficiency attained by the units under his command enabled them to deliver four aggressive and exceptionally successful attacks, the first at Tulagi Harbor on May 4 in which at least eight enemy Japanese vessels were destroyed or severely damaged, and later, on May 7, when an enemy carrier was sunk; both engagements maintained in the face of heavy anti-aircraft fire. Opposed also by fierce fighter attacks on May 8, and firing from extremely short range, Lieutenant Commander Taylor's squadron succeeded in sinking or seriously damaging another enemy Japanese carrier. These actions, carried on in the face of constant and grave danger, contributed materially to the success of our forces in the Battle of the Coral Sea.

Citation for Gold Star in lieu of a second Navy Cross:

For extraordinary heroism as a Torpedo Squadron Commander in action against enemy Japanese forces at Salamaua and Lae New Guinea, on March 10, 1942. In the face of heavy antiaircraft fire and enemy fighter opposition, Lieutenant Commander Taylor gallantly led his squadron in a bombing attack against a Japanese seaplane carrier, located 30 miles beyond the planned objective. Scoring a direct hit on the carrier, he and his squadron not only destroyed the aircraft on deck but disabled the hostile vessel. His skillful airmanship and outstanding courage were in keeping with the highest traditions of the United States Naval Service.

After a tour of shore duty, Joe Taylor assisted in fitting out the *Franklin,* and from her commissioning, January, 1944, served as her air officer. During July and August the ship, with her planes, participated in the invasion of Guam and in strikes against Iwo Jima, in the October operations off Formosa, and in the battle for Leyte Gulf. In both latter operations the *Franklin* was hit by enemy planes. The damage from the Leyte Gulf engagement was severe.

For his work during the Leyte Gulf incident, Joe Taylor was awarded the Bronze Star Medal with the following citation:

For distinguishing himself by heroic and meritorious achievement during action with the enemy on 30 October, 1944, while serving as Air Officer in the U.S.S. *Franklin.* After the ship had been set on fire by enemy aerial attack he directed the removal of burning planes on the flight deck and hangar deck in spite of exploding gasoline tanks and ammunition. His administrative and professional skill contributed to the control of the fires and plane salvage and were at all times in keeping with the highest traditions of the United States Naval Service.

Chaplain Gatlin and I learned only slowly and from others that Joe Taylor already had an outstanding war record. We learned from personal contacts that he was an easy man to work with, a pleasant man to chat with, and a man of somewhat volatile temper. We also learned that Joe had been promoted to executive officer in January, 1945, some two months after Captain Gehres had taken command of the ship.

Les Gehres had as a youngster joined the Naval Militia of New York State at Rochester in 1914. Mobilized with that unit at the outbreak of World War I, April 6, 1917, he was appointed ensign in the Naval Reserve and, having completed the course for Reserves at the Naval Academy, Annapolis, in September, 1918, he received his commission as ensign in the Regular Navy. After several years of routine duty, he reported in January, 1927, to the Naval Air Station at Pensacola for flight training, receiving his wings in August of the same year. Like most naval aviators, he had served continuously with naval aviation since that time, flying fighter planes from the *Langley,* the *Saratoga,* and the *Lexington.* He returned to Pensacola to command a training squadron. At this time he also commanded a stunt team at the All-American Air Maneuvers, Miami, which won the trophy for the best team in aerobatics in 1936. Next he was assigned to staff duty aboard the *Yorktown* and then, in June, 1938, was appointed air officer of the *Ranger.* Having had duty on all the aircraft carriers then in existence, he went as executive officer to Ford Island, Pearl Harbor. Forty days before Pearl Harbor Day he was ordered back to the United States and given command of Patrol Wing 4, later to be expanded to Fleet Air Wing 4.

The citations which accompanied the Legion of Merit Awards indicate the accomplishments of Captain Gehres. Legion of Merit citation:

For exceptionally meritorious conduct in the performance of outstanding services to the government of the United States as Commander of a Patrol Wing and later as Commander of a Fleet Air Wing in action against enemy Japanese forces in the Aleutian Islands. Despite extremely unfavorable weather conditions and limited communication facilities, Commander Gehres directed the operations of his planes with such excellent tactical skill and sound judgement as to enable them to locate, attack and destroy hostile ships and installations, and to provide our forces with vital weather data and detailed information of enemy activities. The expert professional ability and valiant devotion to duty of Commander Gehres greatly contributed to the success of his command in frustrating Japanese plans for the invasion of the Eastern Aleutians.

The Gold Star in lieu of a second Legion of Merit carried this citation:

For exceptionally meritorious conduct—as Commander Fleet Air Wing 4—by his initiative, sound judgement and outstanding leadership initiated and successfully continued sustained air operations from Aleutian Island bases against Japanese installations. His conduct throughout was in keeping with the highest traditions of the naval service.

Although Captain Gehres was in command of the ship, his immediate superior was Rear Admiral Ralph Davison, in command of Carrier Task Group Two with headquarters aboard the *Franklin*. As it happened, Rear Admiral Gerald Bogan was also aboard with his officer staff. Gerry Bogan had no official command but had orders to take command of Carrier Task Group Two immediately after the first strike.

Because I had met Admiral Bogan briefly some time

earlier, and because now he had some leisure, being free, at the time, of actual command responsibility, we had a chance to chat frequently, and became good friends. I had first met him when I was chaplain at the mother air station at Pensacola, and when he was commanding the new air station at Miami. I remembered him particularly because he did not like chaplains—and if I remember rightly, he told me so.

Gerald F. Bogan grew up in Chicago, received an appointment to Annapolis, and was commissioned ensign in June, 1916. It was not until eight years later that he began flight training at Pensacola and was designated naval aviator in March, 1925. Like almost all the old-timers, he flew planes from the *Langley* when that ship was still a converted vessel. He also served aboard the *Lexington* and *Saratoga*, taking command of the latter carrier in October, 1942. Just prior to this command he was in charge of the establishment of the Miami Naval Air Station, and its first commanding officer. It was there that I first met him. Happily, aboard the *Franklin*, our relations became more cordial. I'm sure that we became friends.

For his services in command during widespread operations in the Pacific Area, Admiral Bogan was awarded the Legion of Merit, the Distinguished Service Medal, a Gold Star in lieu of a second Distinguished Service Medal, and the Navy Cross.

Rear Admiral Davison was an Annapolis classmate of Gerry Bogan, but he had been assigned to flight training at Pensacola in 1919 and had won his wings in May, 1920. He too saw duty aboard the *Langley, Saratoga,* and *Lexington*, as well as at many air stations throughout the country. From 1939 he was chief of staff to various aviation admirals in various aviation assignments. He had first taken command of a carrier task group in 1943. For his services in these commands he was awarded the Legion of Merit, the Distinguished Service Medal, and a Gold Star in lieu of a second Distinguished Service Medal.

It was obvious that the command aboard the *Franklin* was a good one to be in trouble with, if trouble was to come. But the *Franklin*, nearly three football fields in length and with a population of about thirty-three hundred, in comparison to the entire Task Force 58, was very small indeed. The *Franklin* was only one of sixteen carriers, and guarding these aircraft carriers were eight battleships, sixteen cruisers, and sixty-three destroyers. When it is realized that under standard operations each ship has a clearance of at least two thousand yards around the compass, it becomes apparent what a vast area was covered by Task Force 58.

Few except admirals could look upon the unit ships and correlate them objectively. Whether it be destroyer, battleship, or carrier, the personnel of any ship assumes that its ship is the center about which all is centered. Only astronomers can take seriously the incredible distances of the universe; the rest of us have trouble enough cutting our planet down to size.

As the firmament of ships furrowed toward Japan, life aboard the *Franklin* grew more settled, patterns began to adjust themselves into structure and routine. The scanners slowly revolved in the red dusk of the radar room; the *blit-blah* from the radio shack told us we were in constant contact with the rest of Task Force 58. But below decks the *Franklin* concerned herself with the mundane round of the job, with food, sleep, people, and laughter.

Her crew referred to her as "Big Ben," but there were some doubts expressed whether she had been named after Ben Franklin. It is Navy practice to name battleships after states, cruisers after cities, and carriers after battles or old ships. Many claimed that she was named after the Battle of Franklin, a minor skirmish of the War Between the States. The truth is that she was named after Admiral Farragut's flagship in which he made a tour of European ports after the Civil War, and that ship was named after Ben Franklin; so, at one remove, we did bear old Ben's name.

Ben Franklin would have approved of our scientific hobbyists. Each evening just at sunset, when the day's work was done and no danger threatened, a group of us looked for the "Green Flash." Except at sea in the Pacific, I have never seen it, and then only when the atmosphere was extraordinarily clear. Owing to the refraction of the sun's rays at the horizon and the absorption of the violet and blue wave lengths, just as the sun is sinking below the horizon with an apparent diameter of about two feet, there appears for a brief second a green flash with an apparent diameter of about eight inches. Some astronomers say that those who witness the "Green Flash" (or Green Ray as it is sometimes called) should report their impressions to an astronomical journal. But it is my opinion that the last word has been said by Jules Verne in his story "The Green Ray." Of course, the astronomers and I have differed before. The Scots lass Helena refused to marry anyone until she had seen the Green Flash—the flash which, according to an old Highland legend, once seen, prevents all deception in love because of the magical power it gives of seeing clearly both one's own heart and the hearts of others.

If the astronomers are dissatisfied with this explanation of the "Green Flash," surely they will not contest a still older proverb which takes it as a symbol of fair weather:

> Glimpse you e'er the green ray,
> Count the morrow a fine day.

CHAPTER THREE

The Last Mass

O N THE 17th of March at midafternoon, about the time when "New York's Finest" were leading the parade down Fifth Avenue toward the reviewing stand at the Cathedral of St. Patrick, some twelve hundred boys gathered in the fo'c'sle section of the *Franklin*. It was not a St. Patrick's Day celebration. But, no doubt, from many an Irish heart came a prayer to honor their patron and to ask his protection. The boys were gathered there for prayer. They were attending Mass, and not a Sunday Mass or a Mass of obligation. Yet every Catholic aboard was present. Some who had been scheduled for watch at that hour had exchanged watches with Protestant boys so that each could be present at his respective religious service. For some it was their heavenly patron's feast; others had for patron St. George or St. Boniface, Sts. Cyril and Methodius, Santiago or the patron saint of any of half a dozen other nationalities. But whatever their ancestry they were Americans. The heavenly patroness of America is our Blessed Lady, and on this Saturday a Mass in her honor was to be said.

Twelve hundred American boys crowded the fo'c'sle area, boys ranging from seventeen years up. Boys from every section of the country, from small towns and big cities, from Minot, North Dakota; from San Francisco, California. Some were college men, graduates of professional schools, doctors and lawyers. Some were quite unlettered. Officers and enlisted men, pilots and mechanics, seamen and radio technicians—the whole assemblage of rates and ranks, lowest to highest, was there on the fo'c'sle. Steward's mate stood next to doctor, apprentice seaman beside experienced aviator. A cross section of the ship was there, more than a third of the ship's complement of men.

They were attending Mass before combat. Tomorrow before dawn the first offensive attack would be launched.

In the most forward section of the fo'c'sle were two canvas sheets, big enough to serve as sails for rather large ships. They billowed in the wind as did once the thwart-set sails of Norse ships. The canvas shielded headwinds from two mess tables. On one table, priestly vestments for Mass were laid out. The second table was the altar. Through millions of Masses and centuries of years the altar has always been a table or a tomb. Thus through the ages has been perpetuated a double remembrance, the institution of the Eucharist and the burial of our Lord.

Death, even at Mass, even before combat. But different from the usual horror and bitterness of death. "Eat, drink, for tomorrow we die!" How different the symbolism of the altar and the cynicism of Horace! Food and death, but both in Christ. The cloth which covered the table at His Last Supper, and the winding sheet in which he was embalmed, both are symbolized by the linen altar cloths secured against the wind by thumbtacks. In the most forward part of the ship, and raised well above the deck, this mess-table altar, mystical symbol of table and tomb, a holy mountain where Jesus transfigures and immolates himself, is at once Tabor and Calvary. Twelve hundred men gathered to witness the Transfiguration and the Immolation.

The second table contains the appurtenances which the priest will use at Mass. The glistening chalice and the paten, a saucer of gold upon which the bread for Consecration rests. In ancient years, much larger, it held all the gifts collected in the offerings. But no saucer can contain the offering of this Mass, the voluntary offering of twelve hundred lives. The corporal, a small linen napkin upon which will rest through the solemn parts of the Mass the consecrated Host, our Lord Jesus Christ. And the chalice veil. It hides from view, except at the height of the mysteries, both chalice and paten, as this day hides the near but mysterious tomorrow.

On the table also are the priest's vestments. In donning these, he covers his own personality and puts on Christ. Each garment is rich in remembrance of struggle and death.

The amice, a helmet spiritually more protective than any steel helmet. "Place O Lord, the helmet of salvation on my head to resist the attacks of the devil."

The alb, a white garment, symbol of the pure of heart. "Make me white, O Lord, and purify my heart, so that being made white in the Blood of the Lamb, I may deserve an eternal reward." Blood will flow soon in the white heat of battle, and out of this, what? Eternal life out of death, for those who die. For those who live? At least, please God, a cleansing of heart.

The cincture, the maniple, the stole. Finally the chasuble, principal vestment of the priest at Mass—a "little house." Clothed in this the priest is close to God, and so he prays. "O Lord, Who hast said, 'My yoke is sweet and My burden light,' grant that I may so carry it as to merit Thy grace." The priest's burden indeed is light: no worldly responsibilities, and untold graces to help fulfill his spiritual obligations.

But the priest considered with his flock? Twelve hundred about to face death, each a special responsibility of their priest who must hope and pray and work and pray again that each of the twelve hundred may be ready for death!

I began vesting for Mass, then looked about for a server. In the front row was Dr. Bill Fox. Bill hesitated to accept because he had not served since school days and thought he had forgotten the Latin responses. Despite some reluctance he was appointed Mass server. There was no fear of undue embarrassment, because priest and doctor had come to know each other well. In the confusion of thousands of new names and faces which became the new world and parish when the priest boarded the *Franklin*, Bill was among the first who had made himself known. Friendship ripens quickly aboard ship, and Bill and I were close friends. The Mass began. Priest and server alternated in the recitation of David's Psalm.

" '*Introibo ad altare Dei*: I shall go unto the altar of God, to God who giveth joy to my youth.' " To the youth of the *Franklin*? It is hard to realize at the moment, that before tomorrow is done some of these youths here present will have entered into eternal joy. Who? How many?

" '*Judica me, Deus*: Judge me O Lord and distinguish my cause from the nation that is not holy.' " There was a challenge. If God is to be on our side, we must be on His.

" '*Ab homine iniquo*: From the unjust and the wicked deliver me.' " Avoiding eternal harm is much more important than escaping physical danger. Our Lord Himself gave apt interpretation to this verse of David: "Fear not him who can harm only the body—fear him who can drag both body and soul into hell."

" '*Confiteor Deo*: I confess to almighty God.' " A reminder that many haven't gone to confession yet! Best speak about general absolution during the sermon. (Am I meditating on the prayers of the Mass or am I wandering into mental distractions? It's sometimes hard to distinguish.) This is perhaps the most important Mass this priest will ever say. I should say it with special devotion. Important? It may well be the last Mass I shall ever say. Strange, isn't it, that one appreciates with abstract clarity that some here present will be dead tomorrow, but one never thinks to include oneself? Perhaps I shall be dead tomorrow. (Now that is a distraction!)

"'*Aufer a nobis, quæsumus, Domine:* Take away from us O Lord our iniquities that we may enter into the holy of holies with pure hearts.'" The altar as a symbol of heaven. For some here present, perhaps for me, the symbol will soon give way to reality. With pure hearts some of us will soon enter into the eternal holy of holies.

"'*Gloria in excelsis Deo:* Glory to God in the highest and on earth peace to men of good will.'" The peace which the world cannot give, and on this morning is not giving.

"'*Qui tollis peccata mundi, suscipe deprecationem nostram:* Who takest away the sins of the world hear our prayer.'" Should we pray to come out alive from combat? Surely not that. It somehow doesn't seem right to pray just for that. Prayer to get to heaven? Ultimately every prayer is directed toward heaven. But why not a specific prayer in this Mass that we have grace and strength in the coming battle to do as good a job as possible for God and country? No matter what happens to ourselves.

"'*Munda cor meum:* As once You cleansed with a burning ember the lips of Isaias, the prophet, now cleanse my heart and lips that I may be worthy to preach Your Gospel.'"

It's time to interrupt the Mass, time to preach. As never before, the priest needs God's help to preach Christ well. To tell these boys, and in the telling make them appreciate that if Christ be with us nothing else matters. Or better, if we are with Christ, everything else will fit into proper place: combat, danger, death, even victory. The priest must preach well the Gospel of Christ to his flock on the fo'c'sle. No formal sermon, a heart-to-heart talk about prayer and religion.

"As we all know, boys, tomorrow morning the fighting starts. We've known that for ten days. And before combat each one of you should go to confession and receive Holy Communion. For the past week, several hours each day have been assigned to hear confessions. The first time that the word was passed you might not have heard it. But you should have heard it the third time or the fifth or the tenth. Each day the line outside the chaplains' office grew longer as more and more took advantage of the opportunity of confessing. Today the line stretched half the length of the ship. Yet there are still several hundred who have not yet received absolution. You were warned not to wait till the last day. Well, this *is* the last day, the last day before action. Too many waited too long."

The congregation stood in massed formation, their bodies a blur of faded dungarees, mottled gray and khaki shirts. Faces were attentive, feet shifted ill at ease under the partial reprimand. The priest doesn't know by face or name those who have not been to confession; he knows only the total number of confessions heard and the total of Catholics aboard. But perhaps the conscience of Mike Stepkovitch is bothering him. Perhaps he recalls a similar or stronger reprimand from the Polish pastor when Mike was a lad in the coal-mine district of Pennsylvania. Perhaps Mike promised his mother he would get to the sacraments every week. He forgot. And now it is too late.

Jim Patterson takes the reprimand to himself personally.

The last mail bag which left the ship at Ulithi carried a letter to his wife. The letter told of a new chaplain aboard who reminded him of the curate at St. Anne's in Jamaica. Jim had intended to go to confession immediately after sending his letter, but he delayed and then he forgot. And now it was too late.

Bill Birchall feels good. The reprimand doesn't apply to him. He is glad he went early when the line was short so he didn't have to wait long. But standing next to Bill is Ed Dempsey. He feels very uncomfortable. He shifts from one foot to the other. Everybody aboard couldn't help knowing that Ed was a Dodger fan. He spent half his free time reading about the Dodgers, and the other half talking about them. But when he was a member of the Knot Hole Club back in Brooklyn, he never became so absorbed in baseball that he forgot confession on Saturday afternoon. And here he was, thirteen thousand miles away from Brooklyn and only one hundred miles away from Jap airfields where Kamikaze planes were based. Ed had forgotten to go to confession! Now it was too late!

The priest's instruction to his flock continued. "These remarks are not a reprimand; they are merely a statement of fact. But reprimand or no, it is also a fact that each one of you should receive absolution and go to Holy Communion today. Fortunately, there is available the privilege of General Absolution. Therefore pay attention now to the requisite conditions. Obviously, to be effective, general absolution presupposes that you are sorry for any sins you might have committed. If I am not sorry for having offended God, then not even God Himself can forgive me. General absolution also requires that at the earliest convenience each one will go to confession in the regular way and tell all sins committed since the last regular confession. This is required even though the sins will actually be forgiven at the moment of general absolution. But because your sins are forgiven, then at the regular time during Mass today each one here can and should go to Holy Communion. To guarantee our sincerity let us say out loud together now the Act of Contrition."

On the fo'c'sle of the *Franklin* twelve hundred subdued voices joined in unison, reciting phrase by phrase the solemn and familiar prayer:

> "O my God, I am heartily sorry
> For having offended Thee.
> I detest all my sins
> Because I dread the loss of heaven
> And the pains of hell;
> But most of all
> Because they offend Thee, my God
> Who art all good
> And deserving of all my love.
> I firmly resolve with the help of Thy grace
> To confess my sins, do penance
> And amend my life. Amen."

The special public-address system carried clearly to twelve hundred men the priest's words pronouncing General Absolution: " 'Ego auctoritate Ipsius vos absolvo a peccatis vestris in nomine Patris et Filii et Spiritus Sancti.' "

The eyes of twelve hundred men seemed to mirror the peace which comes with Sanctifying Grace. Mike Stepkovitch, Jim Patterson, Ed Dempsey could not repress a soft smile, reflection of how good they felt. There were one hundred Mikes, Jims, and Eds.

The informal instruction continued with the topic of prayer. The priest told his boys that somehow it did not seem quite logical for the prayer to be principally a request that we come out of the fight alive. The task force was initiating an offensive operation. We were deliberately going into danger in order to force the fight. If our principal objective was to remain unscathed, that could have been done best by staying at Ford Island. We did not want to avoid battle; we were looking for it. Hence, the proper prayer should be to ask God's help for this: that while in the fray we might do as good a job as possible for God and country. "That, my shipmates and my brethren, is the intention for which this Mass today is being offered. God bless you all."

The sermon is finished. The Mass continues. The familiar prayers acquire deeper meaning:

" 'Receive, O Holy Father, almighty and eternal God, this spotless host, which I, Thy unworthy servant, offer unto Thee my living and true God, for my countless sins, trespasses and omissions; likewise for all here present—' " for Datzman and Di Palma, for Grata and Greco, for McCauley, McDonald, and Sokotowski; for Bill Fox who as acolyte participates most closely in the Mass—" 'for all here present that it may avail both me and them to salvation unto life everlasting.' "

At the *Orate, fratres,* the priest turns and addresses the congregation. " 'Pray, brethren, that my sacrifice and yours may be well pleasing to God the Father Almighty.' " To which the server responds in his own name and in the name of all the others: " 'May the Lord receive this sacrifice at thy hands, to the praise and glory of His name, to our own benefit and that of all His holy Church. *Suscipiat Dominus sacrificium de manibus tuis . . .* ' " Dr. Fox struggles through the Latin phrases, jerking them like a schoolboy, half stuttering the difficult syllables. (It's a hard prayer to say, Bill, even when it's recited frequently. It's the *pons asinorum* for those aspiring to be altar boys. The *Suscipiat* prayer is a tongue twister. You were worried about it. That's the real reason you hesitated to act as server. I know, Bill, but I'm glad I was insistent. You said the prayer as well as anyone would.)

The worries of the acolyte are over. Through the more solemn parts of the Mass the priest prays alone, his assistant merely kneeling at attention.

The priest turns back toward the altar. Twelve hundred faces watch, more attentive perhaps than ever before, more aware perhaps of the sublimity of the Sacrifice of the Mass.

In externals, at least, this Mass is different from any they have attended in their churches at home. Here there is no church. Here the fo'c'sle of a warship is church. Rollie Baca sees the little adobe church built in Spanish style, in far-off Albuquerque. There the Mass server was usually a little Mexican boy. Tony Bosco remembers the church in downtown Detroit, where you see the main altar from any seat on three different floors. It's a beautiful church too—and here on the fo'c'sle there are only a table and a canvas backdrop acting as a windbreak. Don Simpson recalls that this is St. Patrick's Day, and there comes to his mind's eye St. Patrick's on Fifth Avenue. Its towering spires are dwarfed now by Radio City just across the street. But the spires are no less inspiring because of that. A big cathedral in the very center of the biggest city in the world. How different Mass on the fo'c'sle of the *Franklin* from Mass at the high altar of St. Patrick's!

The priest bends to pronounce the words of Consecration. His chasuble flaps in the wind of the North Pacific. Everyone is still. He kneels, stands, and elevates the Host. Suddenly the differences mean nothing. Steel deck, canvas shields, skimpy combat vestments fade before the one reality that is the Mass, whether said at high altar or at mess table.

CHAPTER FOUR

Carrier in Combat

MARCH 18TH. The first day of combat. Task Force 58 was ringed around its carriers. The work it had to do was to be done by air attack. Today there were two objectives. In the morning our planes were to concentrate on knocking out the Japanese air power by fighter engagements and strikes directly at their airfields. With this objective accomplished, they were to spend the afternoon searching out the crippled Japanese fleet which, according to our intelligence, was hiding at inland docksides.

Some hours before dawn, general quarters was sounded. I made my way as quickly as I could through dimly lighted corridors and blacked-out decks to the bridge.

In the darkness men, clothed for combat and against the cold, were grotesque blobs of black. Bundled in coat and jacket, bulging with life-belt and first-aid kit, hooded with helmet, shrouded in shadow, no one looked quite human, much less recognizable. But Captain Gehres could be recognized. He is the biggest man aboard, and no matter how tired or tense, he stands erect. And the big white cross on my helmet is vaguely visible. So we were not utter strangers when we met.

"Good morning, Captain."

"Good mor—oh, good morning, Padre. Expecting a busy day?"

"Well sir, aboard the *Ranger* I was fairly good at praying away torpedoes. At least I used to claim part credit for some of the near misses. I don't know how I'll make out with Kamikaze."

"They'll be out after us today," said the captain, half to himself. Then, after a pause: "I hope our fighter combat patrol will take care of them and send the suicide planes to eternity a few minutes before they expect it." He paused. "The air group looks good. It looked ragged the first days out of Pearl, and I let them know I thought so. But they're ready now, and should give a good account of themselves."

"They're quieter than other groups I've known, Captain. Eb Parker, I think, is a sobering influence. In temperament and appearance, at least, he's older than most group commanders. The youngsters look upon him as really ancient."

"Hm-m. Where does that put me, Padre?"

I laughed. "Well, sir, in Navy parlance, you're the 'Old Man.' You can draw your own conclusions!"

The captain returned to the main thought. "Parker's group has a chance today to show its stuff."

"I'm going down now, sir, to the ready rooms to say a short prayer with the boys before they take off."

"Well, don't scare them and don't delay them."

"No, sir, I don't believe there's danger of either."

I went back to the after bridge, down the outer ladder to the admiral's bridge level, through the weather-tight door to the inner island. Here shadows were emphasized by the dim red light, but such emphasis of shadow left at least partial visibility.

The captain's warning not to scare the flyers had some point. A chaplain about to visit the ready rooms for a prayer with the pilots, who have already been "briefed," and are now waiting to take off, does not try to build up a dramatic entry. He is living real-life drama. He wants to underplay the part. There is a real danger of failing in his job of offering spiritual help and succeeding only in making everyone uncomfortable. "Go, ye heroes, go to death and glory," might be in place in opera, but this isn't opera. In a way, it's similar to a big football game, but terribly more important. Now, like every other American boy, I grew up with a zest for football, and at a time when Knute Rockne was a name idolized by every lover of the sport. It might seem strange, but it is a fact, that as I worked my way to the ready rooms I thought of Knute Rockne, and wanted to be like him, in a smaller way, but in a very much more important business. In the spiritual realm I wanted to do to and for these lads about to face death what Knute could so well do to and for his squad about to face Army or Navy. I couldn't, I wouldn't be flippant; and yet I shouldn't be too serious. Everyone knew it was serious business, and there was no need of emphasizing the obvious. A sandwich effect seemed appropriate: a light touch, good solid religious meat, and then another light touch.

I went first to Major Bailey's squadron, the Marine fighter pilots. "Hi, Padre. No choir practice today—too busy." Just the perfect remark! The reference was to an Easter choir this squadron was organizing for me, and the banter was just the light touch needed. "O.K., if you insist on canceling choir practice I insist on a compromise. If you won't sing, then at least I'll make you pray. Seriously, fellows, I'm getting around to all the ready rooms to say a short prayer and give general absolution. This absolution is for the Catholic boys but we'll let you non-Catholics in on it—guaranteed not to hurt! You all know the Lord's Prayer; let's say it quickly but reverently: 'Our Father . . . Thy kingdom come. . . . Thy will be done . . . forgive us our trespasses . . . deliver us from evil.' And now the Act of Contrition." I recited the prayer aloud, and here and there throughout the ready room a voice would catch up the familiar phrases, a boy would join in and not realize he was praying aloud: "'My God, I am heartily sorry for having offended Thee, and I detest all my sins . . . most of all because they offend Thee, my God, Who art all good and deserving of all my love. I firmly resolve . . . to amend my life. Amen.'" And then, amidst a solemn silence, the words of absolution, which the priest pronounces, not in his personal capacity, but in the name of and by the authority of Jesus Christ, "'*Ego . . . vos absolvo*: I absolve you from your sins in the Name of the Father and of the Son and of the Holy Spirit, Amen.'"

No matter what the faith of these boys—in the case of some there is very little faith, in the case of others there is a sincere adherence to some Protestant sect—all join with their Catholic shipmates in an appreciation of the importance of this moment of prayer. As one of the lads told me after the action: "I don't know much about your ceremonies nor about this general absolution, but I flew my plane off the deck with a vague realization that spiritual accounts had been properly settled. I had fixed everything right with God, and therefore everything was all right."

I want the boys to be deeply impressed but I don't want them to confuse religion with pious emotion. I don't want to leave them on an emotional plane. So: "O.K., fellows, it doesn't take long to say a sincere prayer. Now I'll take over that part of the job; from now on you concentrate on your specialty. I want you to do a good job. Good luck, and

Godspeed—and don't shout yourselves hoarse over your 'splashes'; remember, we can't postpone that choir rehearsal indefinitely."

As I left the ready room I fulfilled my promise and said an extra prayer that these lads of mine would be successful in "splashing" the enemy, and that they themselves would not be shot down.

Leaving the Marines, I went to the Navy Fighter Ready Room. Here was the squadron commanded by Lieutenant Commander Kilpatrick. An outstanding fighter pilot himself, he had trained a squadron that gave promise of being outstanding. I made again the same effort to combine solemnity and lightness. Next, I went to the bomber pilots and the torpedo squadron. And then to my special kids, the enlisted fliers, rear-seat gunners, bombardiers and radiomen—the dungaree aviators, youngsters in the enlisted ranks who take all the risks and don't always get their share of the glory. But they got their full share of prayers. If time had allowed a visit to only one ready room, I think I would have gone to them. Happily, though, I knew the flight schedule, and took care to visit all the ready rooms in the order of their departure.

But I had not seen Eb, Commander E. B. Parker, the air group commander in charge of all the squadrons. A visit to his office was routine practice every morning during general quarters. His yeoman Kasch made excellent coffee. In fact, the coffee was so good, and the company so enjoyable, that when the "Secure from general quarters" signal was sounded at sunrise, I would make another visit for another pre-breakfast cup. This morning battle stations were not routine; all the more reason, then, for wanting coffee. Besides, I wanted to see Eb before he took off. I had a St. Christopher medal he had asked me for several days earlier. I hadn't forgotten, but I had delayed delivery long enough. My Navy life has taught me that there are very many non-Catholics, particularly aviators, who have a devotion to St. Christopher. Actually, I have a quarrel to settle with St. Chris on the score of aviation, as I now told Eb.

Sipping my coffee, I gave him the medal. "Eb, St. Chris is a very revered saint and a fine fellow, but just between ourselves I think he has a nerve horning in on aviation." Eb had long since become accustomed to my habit of starting a conversation as if I were in the midst of a riddle. The expression on his long, deceptively solemn face changed not one whit; he sipped his coffee, grunted and waited. "My gripe is this. By formal decree, Our Lady of Loretto is supposed to be the official heavenly patroness of aviators, and either St. Chris is trying to horn in, or he doesn't yet know that the election is over and the votes are all counted."

"Now look, Padre, don't get me in the middle—I'm just a simple Protestant who always wears a St. Christopher medal. And thanks for this one."

"O.K., Eb. God bless you, and may St. Chris bring you back safely. But I still insist he is not the patron of aviators."

Conversation such as this could not, I believe, take place outside the armed forces. Here there is a camaraderie and an understanding which civilians do not share. It seems to me that civilians are much too ill at ease about religious matters, and particularly about differences of religious faith. I don't like being ill at ease. In the Navy, while we sometimes argued about religion, we did have a fundamental understanding and respect for the religious sincerity of our friends. These friends of mine—and many of them are non-Catholics—know me for a Catholic priest; they know I'm sincere about it, that I don't wear my religion on my sleeve, that I appreciate a little banter which some stuffy people might think irreverent. It isn't irreverent. I can banter about heavenly things precisely because heaven is so important to me, as a man banters more about his wife, the greater his affection for her. Chaffing the things we love and feel deeply about is not, perhaps, recommended for every occasion, but it is a very old sport and a natural and very human reaction.

As if to confirm the truth of these reflections, Dr. Sam Sherman now entered Eb's office to pay his respects, wish Eb well, and drink Eb's coffee. Sam was one of the few officers on the *Franklin* whom I had known prior to my reporting aboard. He had come into the Navy shortly after Pearl Harbor, giving up an active practice in San Francisco. Because he had known me of old, and because a chaplain named Joseph Timothy O'Callahan was so obviously a Catholic priest, and because, being a Jew himself, he saw that no one could take offense, Sam had nicknamed me "Rabbi Tim." In unofficial, confidential moments, my close friends aboard would call me "Rabbi Tim." Another example of easefulness about religious matters.

Sam didn't drop into Eb's office merely for coffee. As air group flight surgeon, he looked out for the health of all the aviators. Commander Parker, just now, was his special concern. Eb had a bad head cold, and high-altitude flying doesn't mix well with head colds. But no amount of sniffles would keep Eb grounded on the day when his air group was making its first strike against the enemy.

The conversation in Eb Parker's office drifted into an evaluation of current events. During the night the fleet had closed to one hundred miles off Kyushu. Through the hours of darkness Jap planes had been searching the area. Our radar had detected them, sometimes one, at times as many as twelve. The night-fighter group from the *Independence* was also airborne through the night, but they did not attack. Attack would have revealed our position.

"Why don't the Japs drop flares? They don't need radar to find a fleet this size."

"Don't ask me, Sam. I have my hands full directing my pilots without being responsible for what the Japs do or don't do."

Only those who understand the working of the Jap mind can explain why their search planes did not drop flares. Our force spread for fifty miles across the ocean. A flare dropped anywhere in that area would have revealed at least one ship.

I had a twofold interest in their conversation: normal curiosity to know as much as possible about the action, and a news reporter's zest to gather all items of interest to his audience. I was to be the newscaster during the day on the ship's public-address system. Aboard a warship it is not uncommon for a chaplain to act as spot announcer during action. The purpose of such newscasting is not to make a game out of war, but rather to bring the war directly to the thousand-odd men whose battle stations are below deck. By keeping them informed they become a closer part of a unified fighting team. So it happened that my battle station was the bridge, with freedom of movement throughout the ship as I saw fit. During action my specific but very secondary duty was to stand by observing and absorbing and, when convenient, to broadcast a running commentary on the battle.

This was not a new assignment. It was an old assignment on a new ship. Long ago on the *Ranger*, during the invasion of North Africa, Cal Durgin had suggested such a broadcast. A chaplain's job in battle is to soothe the wounded, minister to the dying, pray with and for the aviators about to fly into battle. It was always agreed that religious duties had priority. But when I was not in the professional role of a priest I would be an amateur newscaster.

We had hashed over the night's developments, and it was time for me to move on. As I left the office, Sam was treating Eb with whatever cabalistic concoction flight surgeons use to make aviators react as if they enjoyed head colds at high altitudes.

"Pilots, man your planes! Pilots, man your planes! Secure wheel chocks and all loose gear about the deck. Stand by to start engines."

I hurried up to the bridge, arriving there to hear the "bull horn" blare the order, "Start engines." The bull horn, a huge loudspeaker, magnifies the sharp tones of the human voice and makes commands audible on the flight deck despite the roar of engines.

On the bridge the light of approaching dawn made individuals somewhat visible. What had been a chunk of darkness now was Henry Hale, the air officer, peering tensely down at the ordered confusion of his command scurrying about the flight deck. But it wasn't really daylight yet— you could still see blue flame shoot from engine exhausts as the planes warmed up. You could also see a few stars— but too few for any promise of a cloudless day.

To get away from the noise of thirty roaring engines, I stepped into the navigator's chart room. My presence in this busy and confined space was tolerated principally because of my role as broadcaster.

The chart showed our present position, less than one hundred miles from the mainland of Japan, less than one half-hour flying time for our fighter and bomber planes to the Jap airfields at Kagoshima and Izumi on the island of Kyushu.

The assistant navigator made a last check of the predicted position of the ship ninety minutes hence. In ninety minutes the planes of our first flight would return to the carrier. In those ninety minutes the ship would travel some forty-five miles, but not in any one direction for very long. At the end of ninety minutes she would have to conform exactly to "point option" so that the returning planes could find her. It's no easy job to navigate a carrier.

The ship turned into the wind; twenty knots blew over the deck, twenty-five knots, thirty-two. The bull horn blared the signal " Launch planes."

The bridge offered a good view of Fred (Red) Harris, flight-deck officer. Faster and faster he rotated his checkered flag, faster and faster propellers whirled and engines roared, until the roar peaked to the frenzy of a whine. "Thumbs up" from the pilot, and a vigorous nod. The signal flag snapped to rest, pointed forward. After thousands of carrier launchings, Red's ear had acquired a peculiar sensitiveness. In the whining roar he could distinguish the purr of a slick-functioning engine. His hand, too, had acquired a special eloquence of gesture which would be the envy of an artist. When Red rotated his flag, engines seemed compelled to "rev" in harmony; when Red snapped that flag horizontally forward, planes shot straight down the center of the deck as though he had jerked a leash.

Parker's plane was first. Airborne just before reaching the end of the runway, straight for a second till clearly free of the ship, then an easy turn to starboard, for thus the slip-stream down the deck was broken. Twenty seconds later Parker's wing man was airborne. At the same interval the others followed until a deck-load of planes was in the air.

With the last plane launched, the ship changed course.

Escorting ships, cruisers, destroyers, obeying the signal flags whipping in the breeze, also turned in precise formation.

Our plane launchings followed "deck-load" tactics. Minutes are precious in modern warfare, both for ship and for aircraft. The first planes off the deck waste valuable gasoline while, circling, they wait for the rest of the group to join formation. Hence it's better, when the task force has many carriers, to launch thirty planes from each and let them join up and be off to the enemy objective. Meanwhile, other planes are readied for the next strike. In addition, the ship can check its onward rush to the enemy coast line. Steaming at thirty knots straight at the shore closes the distance all too rapidly.

The moment that the last plane of the first strike has been launched, preparations are made for the next strike. The piercing noise of engines has given way to a multitude of lesser noises. Bells clang warning; a vast area of the flight deck disappears. In a very few seconds the elevator reappears carrying a plane from the hangar deck.

Visibility is good now as sunrise approaches. It's fascinating to watch the flight-deck team rush about in orderly bedlam. Decked in bright-hued jerseys and helmets, they catch the eye and seem incongruous aboard a warship where everything else is painted a dull gray. The bright hues are not for aesthetic effect. On the flight deck, where the human voice cannot compete with the noise of engines, specialized gestures and specialized colors have been developed to communicate ideas. In the busy medley below, yellow-jersey boys are plane handlers. By hand or tractor they push or pull the planes off the elevator and bring them to their allotted spots on the flight deck. Red-jerseys check the gasoline; other red men stand by with fire extinguishers. Green-jerseys crawl under the belly of the plane, check the bomb attachments. Other ordnance men check the ammunition of machine guns in the wings. When planes are being spotted the flight deck is a very busy and very colorful place.

The routine went on all day. Load after load of planes was lifted to the flight deck, revved and launched. Then the tensing wait while the ship on her new tack sped to the prearranged point where combat-scarred planes expected her.

We could see them come in, a number of specks in the distance, but how important that number was! Our losses, though, on this first day of combat, were remarkably light, and the job did get done.

All morning we pounded their airfields and shot down their interceptors, until we could conduct the afternoon's search practically unchallenged. In the late afternoon a flight of returning planes reported a discovery of what were certainly ships under camouflage in a hidden bywater. The report was soon confirmed by photographic reconnaissance; but darkness was closing in, and the strike at them would have to wait for morning.

That strike would be primarily the *Franklin*'s responsibility. We were the only ship carrying a newly developed weapon for use against naval vessels, the powerful "Tiny Tim" rockets. These rockets were expected to be able to penetrate the toughest steel; one of them could disembowel a ship. The planes from the *Franklin* would carry them by the score tomorrow.

It had been an exhausting day, and tomorrow might be worse. I went to bed soon after sundown, but I was not to sleep.

Time and time again the dim bunk rooms rattled awake to the sound of loud alarms, then a voice over the speakers: "This is not a general alarm. Repeat: This is not a call to battle stations. Let all gun crews man their stations immediately." All except the unfortunate gunners might go back to sleep, if they could, knowing that somewhere above them in the blackness enemy planes were circling, eager to revenge the cruel losses we had inflicted on them.

The first time I was awakened by such an alert, I began a three-cornered debate with myself. My weary old bones told me I needed sleep; my priesthood offered split advice. It told me I could not man a gun; but it also told me that I should be present where there was danger. The debate was finally settled by my sense of common decency, which told me that the youngsters who were called to stations were just as tired as I. So I heaved myself out, scrambled into my gear, and groped my way topside.

I found Captain Gehres sitting in the darkened, glass-enclosed bridge.

"No rest for the wicked, Les. What's happening?"

"Bogies. They must have flown in reinforcements from the north. Joe Taylor is down at C.I.C., and reports quite a few of them circling. Thank God, they don't use flares."

I didn't want to stand around forcing Gehres into unwanted conversation. He had enough on his hands. I went down to C.I.C., Combat Information Center.

Here the lights are always dim, for here are the wraith-colored radars. A bank of screens against one bulkhead glowed palely on the pale, tense faces of the watchers. Not much talking here, but plenty of cigarette smoking: nervous puffs, deep inhaling.

We were being closely shadowed. Unidentified planes, many of them certainly enemy, were out there in the darkness stalking us. The way they kept appearing and reappearing on the screens was ominous. They surely knew our position, or did they?

I could see Joe Taylor in communication with the bridge,

as he was continually throughout the night. It was a difficult decision for Captain Gehres and his executive to make. Should a call to battle stations be issued? If an attack was to come, that was certainly the only course. But there was a difficult day's work to be done tomorrow. A useless expenditure of energy could not be tolerated even for reasons of caution.

This was the reasoning behind the repeated alerts. They were a sort of compromise: The guns were manned against the possibility that one of those blips of light on the radar screen would suddenly become a loud, death-dealing reality roaring out of the night across our flight deck. And yet the majority of the ship's complement still got what uneasy sleep they could, before the renewed stresses of another day's combat.

I returned intermittently most of the night to the taut atmosphere of C.I.C. With some weariness to myself I solved my personal problem, and every time I heard the alert that roused the gunners from their sleep, the chaplain, who could not man a gun, at least got up.

Along about 0200 things quieted down. All not on routine watch were to get back to bed. I gratefully looked forward to at least an hour and a half's uninterrupted nap.

"All hands to general quarters! Man all battle stations! Man all battle stations!" The loudspeaker rasped the order to every compartment throughout the ship. Bugles replaced the quartermaster at the microphone. Speakers amplified the sharp tattoo of the bugle calling, "All hands to general quarters." The strident notes penetrated the deepest sleep of the heaviest sleeper and brought him to consciousness, alert at three-thirty in the morning. But the bugle sounded its call without the accompanying clang of the alarm bell. It was not an enemy attack. It was the call to battle stations as scheduled in the plan of the day. However, it was the call to combat.

A dim light sufficed to get clothes and gear; the less light in the room, the more quickly would eyes become adapted to the darkness of the weather decks. This was not the occasion to make practice runs along new routes from room to bridge during blackout. I took the easiest and most familiar path. My room was only around the corner, five steps from the port-side fo'c'sle door. I passed through the light locks to the weather deck. The night was dark. I knew my way about, but kept my hand before my face and glasses lest I be mistaken. Five steps to port, one aft, about face, left hand reaches for the guide line, the foot feels for the first step of the ladder to the gallery level. At fourth step bend low: even though my head is well protected by my helmet, a collision with the steel overhead is unpleasant. Turn at the top of the ladder, and go port side again, then another overhead beam, and just beyond that a careful step—high scupper—or suffer a painful shin bruise. Through the alley, up two steps—another high scupper—and I'm on the port catwalk which runs along and just below the level of the flight deck.

It was dark. Dawn wouldn't come for an hour; it would be more than two hours before the sun would rise. It was cold. The weather off Japan is not cherry-blossom weather this morning.

Though I could see nothing, I knew the approximate position of the small-caliber guns which jut from the catwalk. I bump into solid blackness which evolves into the dark, heavy-weather clothing of a gunner on watch. "Sorry, lad." His eyes are better attuned to the darkness.

"O.K., Padre." Calm, almost bored. He has stood watch since midnight. The repeated alarms have become routine to him. Those who stand, armed and ready under the open sky, find night alarms much less nerve-racking than those who start awake in cramped bunk rooms below decks. And after all, we had not been attacked; perhaps we would not be.

I went around to the ready rooms before the first strike, which was launched about 5:30. Another strike was scheduled for about 7:00. Around 6:00 I visited the ready rooms and then decided to go to the wardroom, intending to get in a quick breakfast while the second strike was being launched and before the first returned.

I dropped by my room and shed my battle gear, a practice decidedly not recommended during combat. But below decks everything was so familiar, the routine so reassuring, one could easily think that this was just an ordinary operational day.

Lieutenant Red Morgan, senior machinist in charge of all operations on the hangar deck, and Tommy Greene, the senior engineer, along with the few other officers, were eating a hurried breakfast—fried bread, our contemptuous name for French toast.

We discussed the disturbances of the night before, but very briefly. We didn't have much time to waste at breakfast. Time enough, however, to remind Tom Frasure, steward'smate first class, on duty in the pantry, that we did not like fried bread—especially cold. Frasure grinned a reply that neatly sidestepped our complaint about the temperature of the meal, "That ain't fried bread, sirs; that's French toast."

Then it came.

CHAPTER FIVE

This Is It!

THIS IS *it!*

No doubt about it! How many times aboard carriers had some unscheduled explosion alerted my mind with the thought "This *may* be *it*"? How many times had I speculated how fast or slow I'd be to realize "it" when "This *may be*" changed to "This *is!*"

But when "*it*" strikes, there is no doubt. Quicker than an echo of the blast the mind knows that the moment has come.

Was it a Jap, a Kamikaze, or one of our own bombs? A Tiny Tim?

Another *Bang!* An echo or another explosion?

I sprawled on the deck of the wardroom. I suppose Gats, Tommy Greene, Red Morgan, and the other officers who seconds ago had been listening to me sound off on French toast flung themselves to the deck as I did. I don't remember. Those first moments were given over to instinct, the mad clutch for life. I crouched underneath a table, inconsequentially shielding my head from bits of glass which pelted from broken light fixtures. Hundreds of tons of high explosives ready to blow up, and I shielded my head from bits of glass! But I followed blind instinct only for a split second until my mind focused.

"This is *it!*"

One hundred planes crowded the flight and hangar decks, each plane with gas tanks filled to capacity, thousands of gallons of high-octane gas ready to burst into flame. And bombs—one-thousand- and two-thousand-pound bombs—were attached to the planes, were stacked in various compartments throughout the ship. And rockets, on the flight deck, on the hangar deck, on the deck below, on this deck!

Sudden death was everywhere, for everyone, for the whole ship; death by fire, explosion, disintegration.

I forgot the tinkling glass of broken light fixtures, and remembered the words of absolution: "Dominus Noster Jesus Christus vos absolvat." May Our Lord Jesus Christ forgive you! "Ego auctoritate Ipsius vos absolvo." And I by His authority absolve you from your sins, in so far as you need and I am able. "In Nomine Patris et Filii et Spiritus Sancti." In the name of the Father and of the Son and of the Holy Spirit.

I finished the general absolution while fragments of broken glass were still falling. Smoke rolled into the wardroom from the portside passageway and from the port and starboard ventilators.

Within twenty seconds more than one hundred men came crowding into the wardroom. But the hundreds who were not here? Where were they? About a thousand worked on the flight deck and gun mounts. If their post was too dangerous, they had the refuge of the open sea. All the others were inside the ship where every compartment was now a potential tomb.

About three hundred had duties on the gallery deck; on the hangar deck, besides its working complement of four hundred, there would be another four hundred in the mess line waiting their turn for breakfast; about three hundred would be eating in the various messing compartments on the third deck. Some eight hundred more would be at their posts in the lower decks, in firerooms and engine rooms, in ordnance and control stations. Over 3,200 men were stationed in every part of the ship, and now in every part sudden death was about to strike! There were men who, at this instant, were drawing their last breath.

But for about thirty seconds there were no more explosions.

It was the Feast of St. Joseph, patron of happy death. Death is not horrible if it becomes a gateway to Heaven; death is horrible only if it strikes while one is turned away from God. On his feast day, St. Joseph perhaps has special influence. Was it an answer to prayer, this thirty-second lull?

In our prayers before entering combat, these boys and I had not asked to escape unscathed, to come out alive; we had asked Divine Assistance to do a good job for God and country. We had reminded ourselves that, should death come, in whatever form, it would be a happy death if we died in the friendship of God.

Thirty seconds is not a long time. But it takes much less than that to say a prayer. Even a very quick prayer, a breath of love and sorrow, can be sufficient, especially in conjunction with the priest's administration of the Sacrament of Penance. I repeated the words of absolution, "Ego vos absolvo," for the benefit of those who, however remiss their past, had taken advantage of the thirty seconds to recite a quick prayer.

Only later did I learn that, following the brief interlude, a wall of fire swept the entire length of the hangar deck and left in its wake the bodies of eight hundred dead.

The mind reacts quickly in emergencies. These were my thoughts and prayers as I crawled from under the table and stood in the wardroom with a few of the officers and one hundred enlisted men. There was a mood of intent uncertainty, almost incipient panic. Then a clear command cut through our fear: "All hands stand by until we can find an exit."

We recognized Red Morgan's voice. No drawl now; although calm, it was sharp with authority, sharp enough to cut through dazed minds and compel attention. Good advice, too, and all of us followed it. Whether because we realized it was good, or because it was a command given at a moment when we all needed the bracing of authority, we followed it. And disaster became less shapeless, took on the contours of a job. For the men in the wardroom the work of saving the *Franklin* began when Red Morgan called, "All hands stand by until we find an exit."

Volunteers were sent to explore the various possible exits. I looked around for Tommy Greene, the senior line officer present. He had vanished with the first explosion. Had he tried to get to the Main Engineering Control, his battle station? From the wardroom that is down aft. To reach it he would have to pass what seemed to have been the center of the explosion. I prayed he would make it.

In seconds the messenger returned from starboard aft. No exit there—only smoke and flame. From port aft, the route to the engine room, heavy smoke seeped through a blocked passage. Port side forward was a blind alley. The only exit was a hatch to the hangar deck.

Red's voice again: "To get out, make your way along starboard passage forward and up to the fo'c'sle."

I joined the trek. No one in the wardroom needed help; many topside might desperately need it. This starboard passage on the second deck was very familiar to me; it was my customary route between my room on the fo'c'sle and the wardroom. It is a narrow corridor off which stem many small cubicles which on a warship pass for officers' rooms. It is not a straight passageway partly because it conforms to the general tapering outline of the forward part of the ship, partly because all passageways are designed with offsets or jogs which act as buffers to an explosive blast.

More effective buffers were the two bomb-proof doors which divide the passage into small water-tight compartments. These doors were, of course, closed and, if any blast sprang the hinges, they would remain closed and our only exit would be cut off. We would be in a dead end. And yet, as our group passed through, the doors were carefully closed again. Even at the risk of sealing our tomb, we had been trained always to close battle doors during combat. In the long run it prevents greater damage to ship and men.

Starting from the wardroom we were immediately under the front section of the hangar deck. As we marched, the passage made a sharp right jog where it skirted the pit of the most forward of our three airplane elevators. Because we had been launching planes, I knew the elevator was in the *Up* position, its floor flush with the flight deck. In this position it formed part of the take-off area, its edges locked by heavy steel braces to the fixed flight deck.

The pit extending to the level of the second deck is separated from the corridor along which we had to pass by a thin steel bulkhead. As we reached this part of the passage, the whole ship quivered in a mighty blast. The boys were thrown to the deck, and pitched one against the other.

As in a great storm, disaster had struck with a wild wind, followed only later by thunder and lightning. But this wind was flame, burning gasoline. Starting at the hangar deck, it had burst forward with hurricane speed and more than hurricane fury.

One breath of that wind seared a man's lungs. The hurricane raced on, leaving the hangar deck heaped with corpses. It shriveled planes in its path, while each plane gave new impetus to the storm—three hundred gallons of new impetus —and there were forty planes parked on the hangar deck!

From the burning airplanes tumbled bombs and rockets— hundreds of them—but so swift was the speed of this fiery wind it left them intact. Later, in its wake, slower fires could blow them up. The fire had swept the entire length of the hangar, and hot explosive gases built up pressure in the forward elevator pit.

As we passed Indian-file behind the elevator bulkhead, the open pit, a few inches of steel away, was like a corked retort full of burning gases. Explosive pressure was trapped between the side bulkheads and the heavy elevator locked into the flight deck. Something had to give.

A massive blast shook the entire ship. With a mighty smash the elevator was torn from its locks and pushed eight or ten feet upward. The succeeding vacuum sucked it back, and it fell askew into the pit. The escapees from the wardroom were thrown to the deck. We lost our footing, and we nearly lost our lives. Why hadn't the light bulkhead given way instead of the heavy elevator? At the time we didn't realize how close death had come.

This blast that might have killed us did unsteady our nerves. Men, overanxious to get out of this hot, warped-steel confinement, broke ranks and bunched at the end of the passage. Here a ladder led up to the main deck well forward of the hangar space, and from there another ladder led to the fo'c'sle.

As always in combat, at the top of each ladder the hatches were battened down, and the upper decks were accessible only through the small emergency escape holes built into each hatch. Along the passage two or even three men could walk abreast; up the ladder, two could climb abreast. But the escape hole was a bottleneck. A seaman can hoist himself very quickly up through such manholes; two seamen abreast can never get through the hole together. Bottlenecks during danger lead to panic.

"Here, boys, single file, one at a time through the manhole. Take your turn, Reilly; we'll all get out faster. I'll wait my turn. Now, get in single file."

Because my words were clear and loud they commanded respect and inspired confidence. Yesterday's calm, nondramatic broadcasts were a good preparation. Because of the broadcasts, also, the men recognized my voice.

Calmly and with dispatch our group climbed both ladders and reached the fo'c'sle level, one deck above the main or hangar deck and two decks above the wardroom. The open fo'c'sle was unchanged, encumbered with its usual assortment of anchors, chains, cables, tackle and winches.

Just aft of this open space and on the same level was the junior aviators' bunk room, as well as many officers' rooms, including my own. I took a moment and hurried to my room. There I retrieved the life belt and helmet which should have been with me at all times. The life belt I knew had cracked along the seam and was therefore useless. I regretted then the carelessness of not having replaced it with one in good condition. But there was no time for replacement now. I couldn't run the risk of being misinterpreted. If I should go hunting now for a serviceable life belt, some might conclude that all hope for the ship was gone. This was the first time I realized distinctly that my actions in the present emergency would greatly influence the boys for good or ill. So I fastened the defective life belt and hoped I would not need it.

I was glad, though, I had my helmet. It was a good helmet and could protect my skull from even heavy shrapnel. But it was valuable for another reason, too. Painted in front was a large white cross which would tell everyone who saw it that I was a chaplain. The helmet was a badge of office.

However, even the helmet was secondary. I opened my safe and took out the vial containing the holy oils for the Sacrament of Extreme Unction. And thus, belted with a defective float, helmeted with the cross, carrying the holy oils for the dying, I went in search of my proper work.

The lights were still burning in the junior aviators' bunk room—a large area about 36 by 48 feet. The air was close. There was no smoke, no sign of danger except the pitiful evidence of some thirty badly burned and mangled bodies. They had managed to crawl or had been helped by buddies from the forward port of the hangar deck to this place of relative safety.

Chaplain Gatlin was here, too. This was our place. With the wounded and dying. Were there any doctors? None were around; perhaps none were alive. But Mason, the warrant pharmacist, was here, and with him several pharmacist's mates. The junior aviators' bunk room became an emergency hospital. The corpsmen were the doctors, and first-aid kits supplied the medication—sulfa powder, burn jelly and morphine.

"Gats" and I saw each wounded boy, prayed with him, comforted him as best we could. No more than a minute with each boy, but long enough to give spiritual aid and some mental peace.

Their individual religion? Who knows? And who would ask at such a time?

"Do you want to say a prayer, lad? Let's say the Lord's

Prayer. 'Our Father, Who art in Heaven . . . Thy kingdom come. Thy will be done . . . Forgive us our trespasses . . .'"

Phrase by phrase a dying boy and the priest pray together. The boy on the bed, the priest kneeling beside him, bending over him, resting a hand on a charred forehead or squeezing a hand in a firm grip. We say the "Our Father" and follow it by the "Act of Contrition."

This prayer, too, would be familiar to a Catholic boy, and he would join with me phrase by phrase. From this would I know he was Catholic.

"O my God, I am heartily sorry for having offended Thee, and I detest all my sins . . . most of all because they offend Thee, my God . . . I firmly resolve, by Thy Grace, to do penance, and to amend my life."

The prayer concluded, I give absolution and anoint him with the Sacrament of Extreme Unction.

For some, the Act of Contrition was a new prayer and perhaps, for this reason, even more meaningful. These, who had joined in the recitation of the Lord's Prayer, listened to, and with serious eyes attended, this prayer of sorrow, of perfect love of God. They didn't know the words, but then and there they made it their prayer; they meant every word that was said. Tears came to their eyes, and peace came too. And not a few of those boys, so alert as the prayer was recited, at its conclusion looked up, calm wonder shining in their eyes, and died in my arms. When I die, I hope to go to Heaven and I expect to meet those boys.

But the peace was spiritual and internal only. The conflagration on the hangar deck, having made a holocaust of the planes, now had heated the bombs and the rockets to explosion point. The ship trembled as in a mighty earthquake; the noise of the explosions paralyzed my mind.

Yet another explosion, and another, and another, and another. The lights went out; our bunk-room hospital was illuminated only by dim battle lamps. We would hear a weird and ghostly swish, like the sound of a swift messenger from hell, then another explosion, and another, and another.

"Don't be too frightened, lad; let's go on with our prayers. 'Forgive us our trespasses . . . deliver us from evil.'"

I moved from bed to bed, trying to appear unhurried, trying to pretend that the explosions were only incidental, trying not to show I realized that any second now a "Tiny Tim" might burst through the thin bulkheads separating the hangar deck from this haven of the dying; trying to pray to St. Joseph that this final explosion would not come until each dying boy was spiritually prepared for death.

And so to the next bedside. If only those explosions wouldn't make so much noise! Here in the enclosed bunk room it was only the noise that actually reached us. The rest was left to the imagination. And what a torment to the imagination of the wounded! How awful must be the explosion itself! Young minds strained against sanity.

"Father, are the rockets exploding, the 'Tiny Tims'?"

"Easy, lad. It's probably the twenty-millimeter stuff. Or it may be the forty-millimeter shells. They make a lot of noise when they're fired, and they'll make more noise exploding free."

"It's too loud, Father. It's too loud for that."

"Easy, lad, easy. It's probably only the forty-millimeter stuff."

Morphine soothes bodily pain, dulls the mind, and, perhaps, helps to save sanity. Certainly it saves the chaplain from the temptation to lie.

For the "Tiny Tims" *were* blowing up. A ghastly hiss, then another explosion. Ten, fifteen, twenty of them in as many minutes. I bent low over my patients, shouted into their ears. If the noise *completely* drowned out the prayer, then a boy could feel the pressure of a handclasp and watch the moving lips dimly visible by the light of the battle lamp: "Our Father, Who art in Heaven, hallowed be Thy Name . . ."

Chaplain Gatlin and I continued our ministrations to the dying until we had seen each boy in the junior aviators' bunk room. But here there were less than forty; in other parts of the ship there must be many more still alive, many perhaps wounded and dying. They should be reached if they were accessible.

"Gats" would continue to look after the boys in the bunk room and fo'c'sle. They couldn't be left alone. The more alert among them must have known that there was nothing to prevent a "Tiny Tim" rocket from twisting into that compartment and blowing them all to bits. And they lay helpless on the beds of the bunk room. But "Gats" could keep them calm; for this he had a special gift. I knew because he told me in a quick moment: "Joe, I'm praying just one prayer. 'God, you know I'm afraid, but don't let me show it. My job is to keep these youngsters calm.'" That's a good prayer; only a realist, humble and strong, could make such a prayer. And the prayer was abundantly answered. So I left "Gats" to stay with the boys in the bunk room, and started out to look for others who might need help.

I took the outside starboard passage, the most direct route to the hangar deck. Though daylight made the passage clear, I hugged the bulkhead to keep as far as possible from the rail lest the concussion from some explosion blow me overboard. The noise seemed more terrible now, perhaps because I was not at the moment ministering to others. I proceeded, pressing myself close to the inner bulkhead to take advantage of what protection it might offer. I squeezed past several boys who were just standing in the passage leaning against the bulkhead. In a lull between explosions I spoke to one of them, but the words did not register. His eyes did not focus; his jaw was sagging. I passed along and met another and saw the same dull, almost stupid, expression. Now these boys, as they abundantly proved later, were heroic almost beyond description. But at the moment, though not wounded, they were helpless, and beyond help, momentarily stunned, paralyzed, not, I believe, with fear but with awe. The noise of explosion following explosion, each blast worse than the preceding because of the cumulative horror of what had gone before; the billowing smoke, a shroud mantling a dead ship; the flames, snake-tongued, writhing high into the sky or lashing fore and aft, port and starboard, scourging those who thought themselves safely distant from the center of destruction—all this was truly awe-inspiring.

But there was work to be done, and the awareness of this was as a shield between me and the full terror of the spectacle. The open passage I was in extended for about 250 feet along the side of the ship and led to a platform from which an inboard ladder descended to the hangar deck below. The platform offered a clear view into the hangar deck space. The hangar deck was one massive blaze, not leaping flames, just one solid mass of fire. Here and there, like coals of special brilliance, were airplane engines glowing white hot, glaring so intensely that their image hurt the eye and branded the memory forever. No one was alive in the hangar deck. No one could live a moment there. Save for a quick prayer, I could not help any of those who had died there and whose bodies were already consumed.

The glowing engines, which first caught my eye, were harmless. At worst they could be only secondary missiles. They might hurtle through space propelled by the force of some explosion; they themselves could not explode. But somewhere in that inferno, though I could not see them through the blaze, were real explosives—many two-thousand-pound bombs, more one-thousand-pound bombs—which had been burned loose from the planes in the first fire and were now rolling on the hangar deck waiting to be heated to explosion temperature. But worse than the bombs were the "Tiny Tim" rockets with twelve times the explosive power of our biggest bomb, scores of rockets each one capable of blowing up a battleship, rockets which would not explode where they were lying but would swish in erratic parabolas to bring destruction to any place and every place. The wounded in the bunk room were right to fear the "Tiny Tims" before all else.

Already for half an hour the bombs and rockets had been exploding at the rate of about one per minute. At that rate the explosions would continue most of the day. But a glance into the furnace on the hangar deck made me think the explosions would be much more rapid. There seemed no reason why they should not all explode simultaneously—and now. If they did, the ship would be blown to bits; if they didn't, it would be a miracle.

I did not remain long on this platform looking into the inferno of the hangar deck. It was too dangerous, and there was nothing to be gained by the risk. If I couldn't get down to the hangar deck, then I would try to get up to the flight deck. From the fo'c'sle, I remembered, a ladder goes inboard and up to the gallery deck and thence to the flat top. But flames made this route inaccessible. Offshoots from the solid fire in the hangar licked along the rungs.

To get topside I must retrace my steps to the fo'c'sle and from there hunt for catwalks and ladders and passages that had not been blown out or blocked by fire. The boys whom I had passed previously in the passage came with me to the fo'c'sle. Later they would work with me on the flight deck. Going through the fo'c'sle, I made another trip to my room. I would need my flashlight in the now blackened passages. I took time to smear anti-flash-burn paste over my face and put on the long, anti-flash gloves. Now more than ever, I depended for recognition upon the cross on my helmet.

From the fo'c'sle, up and across an open catwalk, I finally found access to the forward flight deck. Nearly one thousand feet of flight deck and nearly nine hundred feet aflame! Not solid fire as below, but flames, tall as towers, leaping high, snapping in all directions. Smoke swelled to the clouds, rolled along the deck and over the sides. It hung around us like a local overcast, but blacker than the most forbidding day.

The smoke hid the island and its bridge completely from my view. Then a rift in the cloud gave a view of Captain Gehres on the bridge, firm and stern. Behind him was Steve Jurika, navigator. "Why don't they leave the island before they're trapped completely?" When the smoke closed in again, they were still there. Again a rift—the same sight, the same question, and again they didn't leave. Then an explosion. I think I was thrown to the deck. I know I saw shrapnel, entire airplane engines, and untold smaller chunks of steel shooting through the air—hurtling up, then pelting down. More smoke. Was the island still there? Another glimpse of the bridge and of Captain Gehres. This sequence continued intermittently. Each time the smoke lifted, those on the forward flight deck had a glimpse of Captain Gehres;

each glimpse gave the ship the courage born of brave example.

The one hundred feet clear of flame was strewn with bodies: burned bodies, mangled, bleeding bodies; everywhere the stench of burned flesh, the sound of deep groans, the clammy feel of men already dead. This was our flight deck.

Sam Sherman had taken charge here, helped by the ever present pharmacist's mates. I joined them to administer spiritual treatment. The first patient was already dead. I went from one to the next; a prayer, an absolution, an anointing. "Our Father Who art in Heaven . . . I am heartily sorry for having offended Thee. . . . With this anointing may our Lord forgive you all your sins."

It was cold on the forward flight deck, though not as cold as the after-section was hot. If only the elements could strike a happy medium; everything was extreme—extreme cold, extreme heat, and everywhere extreme courage. The cold was uncomfortable for all, even those who could keep their blood circulating by activity; for the wounded the cold was critical. They were in a state of physical shock, and needed warmth to survive their wounds. They must have blankets. Strange for the mind to flash from prayers to blankets. Yet not so strange. The mission of priests, ministers of God, is not confined to spiritual activities. Our Lord also commissioned them to perform the corporal works of mercy. To clothe the naked? Well, certainly to find blankets for the wounded. But where find blankets in this devastation?

The little trouble it had been to gain a detailed knowledge of the ship was well repaid that morning. Between the wounded on the flight deck and the wounded on the fo'c'sle was the forward gallery, where a very large bunk room was located. "Here, lads, you and you and you, go down the forward catwalk—it's clear of fire and smoke—go immediately below to the gallery bunk room. Each of you get two helpers and all of you bring up blankets. If you can't find fifty blankets, bring up mattresses—and quick! Go now, and hurry back."

It would be fitting to give individual credit to the lads whom I thus commandeered. I should like to attest publicly to their alacrity and spontaneity in fulfilling the task so curtly assigned. But at the moment I didn't recognize them, and it was not an occasion for introductions. They were not looking for credit; they were working to help their wounded shipmates as later they were to perform unheralded feats of heroism to save their stricken ship.

I continued ministering to the wounded, continued the prayers, the absolutions, the anointings as blankets and mattresses arrived, enough for all the wounded. At last the doctor and the chaplain had seen each patient. There was a moment's respite. Sam and I rested.

When first we had sighted each other on the forward flight deck we had merely waved, for our respective duties absorbed our complete attention. Yet I think that this wave of the hand meant exactly the same thing to both of us: "Thank God you're alive!" But you don't talk about such things, however deeply you may feel them. Now when we did talk it was about surface, impersonal things. Sam was dazed. Although his medical skill was unimpaired, his mind was dazed. He tried to piece together for me his version of what had happened, but a few of the pieces of the puzzle stayed missing.

On duty as flight surgeon, Sam had been on the flight deck alongside the "island" as our planes were being launched. The roar of engines and whine of propellers blotted out all other sound. He didn't hear the hurried radio warning, "Bogie [enemy plane] reported by visual contact." He didn't hear the captain say, "From Bridge to Radar Plot: check the screen for bogie." Nor did he hear the reply which was the last word from the Radar Room: "Radar to bridge—screen shows no bogie."

Sam couldn't hear any of this. But, looking forward over the ship's bow, Sam could see, about a mile ahead, a small, black, low-ceiling cloud. As our planes leaving the flight deck became airborne, they seemed to choose this cloud as a sky marker for rendezvous. Then out of the black cloud came a plane, a twin-engined plane. She came straight, heading dead for the ship; she came low, beneath the level of our island masts, and fast, better than three hundred miles an hour. So quick that the eye couldn't follow them, two small bombs dropped on the *Franklin*. The first, striking not many feet from where Sam was standing, penetrated flight and gallery decks and exploded in the hangar. The second exploded well astern on the flight deck, a considerable distance from Sam, but not so far that he escaped unscathed. The concussion hurled him against the island structure. Because he remained unconscious unknown minutes, there were a few pieces of his puzzle that would be forever lost. Sam still wondered that he was alive, how he possibly could be alive. He would not have been, if the first Jap bomb, as well as the second, had exploded on the flight deck.

Now chaplain and doctor ministered to each other. Amidst fire and explosion in this moment of respite, the Jewish doctor and the Catholic priest said a prayer together. Then Sam patched a slight gash in my leg. Some minutes earlier, after a particularly bad explosion, I had started searching for possible victims, those who might have been knocked unconscious by the blast and would die unless dragged out of the smoke and flames. As I walked the flight deck, a minor explosion had hurled a hunk of steel between my legs; part of the deck, perhaps, or a piece of an airplane engine. One of the countless secondary missiles which were an incidental source of danger throughout the day. Happily, most of them missed their mark, and this was one of these. It merely scratched the calf of my leg. But it could have been a fatal wound.

By this time a destroyer had maneuvered to windward and closed on our starboard side. With Captain Gehres yelling orders through a megaphone, lines were thrown from them to us, and when the ships were thus secured a breeches buoy was rigged to run across the forty feet which separated the sleek destroyer and the blazing *Franklin*. The admirals and the key officers of their staffs were now being transferred.

The awkwardness of transfer by breeches buoy was symbolic of the awkwardness of the position these officers found themselves in. The *Franklin* was mortally wounded; her chances of survival were slim. But meanwhile the other ships of the task force must carry on the attack against the Japs, and Admiral Ralph Davison and Admiral Gerry Bogan must help direct the attack. Hence they must have quarters where facilities for such direction were available. Their job was to help coordinate and press the offensive; to others belonged the more dramatic but less important task of keeping a dying ship alive. Nevertheless, it is embarrassing for an admiral to be the first to leave a stricken ship; it looks undignified—just as undignified as transfer by breeches buoy. But it is his duty, and he is not swayed from duty by misplaced sentiment as he is swayed by the swinging breeches buoy.

Sam and I watched the transfer for a moment and then

headed for the fo'c'sle to check whether the wounded there were receiving attention. We made the descent from the flight deck by the same forward ladders and passages. The thwartship catwalk on gallery-deck level which gives access to that bunk room where blankets had been found for the wounded forms a sort of balcony overlooking the open fo'c'sle, below and forward. On the fo'c'sle groups of boys, still bewildered, huddled amidst the paraphernalia of chains and anchors and hawsers. Among them were several in officers' blue uniforms. Strange that they should be wearing blue instead of battle khaki; yet more strange that they should be standing listlessly about the fo'c'sle, no less stunned than the enlisted men who have a right to expect leadership from their officers. The explanation of these blue officers' uniforms, when discovered, exonerated the *Franklin's* junior officers of any failure in leadership, but revealed a dangerous confusion which was the direct result of misguided kindheartedness.

Those wearing the blue officers' uniforms were not officers. Some well meaning junior aviator, concerned that the men were wet and cold and frightened, had distributed officers' coats from the aviators' bunk room. He forgot that on the fo'c'sle there was an emergency store of regulation heavy-weather clothing for just such a contingency. He did not reflect that gold stripes on a sleeve were a symbol of officer leadership, not mere decoration. Those stripes implied not only privileges, but responsibility too, and background, training, the right to lead. With divisions disorganized, and faces masked by smoke smears and grease, officers could be distinguished only by their insignia. And now young, enlisted boys were wearing these insignia. Before the day was over these boys proved themselves great heroes; all were ideal followers, and some proved to be natural leaders.

But leadership was not expected of them. It is expected of officers. Any one of these boys could bolt into panic with no discredit, but if, because of his uniform, others assumed he was an officer, the bad example of failure in leadership could easily lead to general panic. By misguided kindness there was added to the ship's troubles this further disorganization. It was a source of confusion throughout the day.

Sam and I proceeded to the bunk room. Chaplain Gatlin was still there; looking after the lads, calming them, cheering them, not in any artificial pietistic way, but solidly, effectively. A few minutes before our arrival he had been helping a wounded boy up to the bunk room from the deck below. They were in the cross-passage immediately in front of the elevator pit when a lot of small-caliber ammunition blew up. The thin bulkhead was peppered with forty-caliber and twenty-millimeter slugs. "Gats" wouldn't leave the wounded lad there alone, and he couldn't make haste with his burden. In the barrage of bullets one spot on the passage was no less dangerous than another. With a quiet prayer, "Gats" continued to assist the lad along the passage as if he had nothing but scorn for slugs of steel. I know "Gats" well enough to realize that he was not trying to be spectacular in this episode. He did not relish a hailstorm of bullets, but found himself in a situation where he had to pretend to scorn them. Only those of us who saw "Gats's" courage in action can appreciate why he so successfully kept the wounded calm.

Also in the bunk room when Sam and I arrived was Doc Smith. Commander Smith, Medical Corps, U.S.N., senior medical officer aboard, had been below decks at the time of the first explosion. Momentarily trapped, he treated the wounded who were accessible. Fortunately for them as well as for him, it was not long before an exit was found, and Doc Smith brought his quota of wounded to the aviation bunk room on the fo'c'sle. Like the bark of a starter's gun, that first explosion had started him working with the wounded and dying in a race against death. He wasn't to stop for three days.

Two other doctors were still unaccounted for: Dr. Jim Fuelling, of Indiana, and Dr. Bill Fox, of Milwaukee. Many hundreds of other officers and men, of course, were also unaccounted for, and we had no means of knowing at the moment whether they were alive or dead.

Dr. Fuelling wasn't dead. He was leading in prayer three hundred boys who were trapped with him in a compartment two decks below the hangar.

They had been trapped in the enlisted men's after mess hall, where the men had been eating breakfast. The first big explosion had blocked every known exit. The fires blazing above and about them made the compartment an oven. Smoke further fouled an atmosphere already vitally short of oxygen. Consciousness of grave peril, the torture of suspense, the impossibility of self-help, and the enforced inactivity provided all the ingredients for panic. Fear gripped one, then another; voices that began in whispers ended in something like screams. But Jim Fuelling squelched the incipient panic: "Quiet, men, quiet!" His voice was high in volume but low in pitch. "We're trapped here for a time, but don't lose your heads. Don't squander your energy. We haven't much oxygen; don't waste it. Breathe quietly. Sit on the deck, say a prayer, let's all say a prayer."

And then Don Gary spoke. Lieutenant Don Gary was an assistant engineering officer up from the ranks, a thin-faced man, bony, homely with a homeliness that somehow reminded you of home, of your father or big brother or perhaps your favorite uncle. Gary knew the ship below decks as a surgeon knows anatomy; he knew every passage and duct and vent throughout the bowels of the ship down to the very bilge. Somewhere in this maze, down many decks perhaps, starboard or port or centerline, by devious junctions and by-passes, there must be a way out of this trap. Gary's voice fits his strong thin face, a quiet voice that carries conviction.

"The doctor's right, men; don't lose your heads. I know this ship. I'll find a way out and I'll be back to get you. I mean that. I'll be back to get you!"

As he stumbled off through the adjoining smoke-filled, bomb-packed compartment, the boys in the mess hall prayed not only for themselves but for Lieutenant Don Gary, for his success in discovering a safe passage through the labyrinth in the bowels of a dying ship. And Doc Fuelling continued his conquest of panic; he continued to lead the boys in prayer.

While Jim Fuelling acted as spiritual leader to the boys trapped in the after-mess compartment, "Gats" and I, the two official chaplains, were exchanging ideas in the emergency hospital on the fo'c'sle. We discussed the prospects ahead of us. By our continued presence together it might have appeared to those who saw us that each needed the other to bolster his courage. Such an interpretation would curtail our effectiveness in calming and encouraging the men, and we wanted to exert what influence we had as effectively and as widely as possible. "Gats" and I agreed that we should not remain together. It's a queer feeling when in the midst of tragedy two friends agree to part, each facing death, each not knowing whether the other will survive, both suppressing the thought that this might be their last meeting, their final parting. It's a queer feeling, but instead of voicing such thoughts you merely remark: "See you later 'Gats'; keep an eye on things here."

With Sam Sherman I began the return trip to the flight deck, using the now familiar route. On the catwalk we met Joe Taylor. In a great hurry, he didn't stop even for a moment. But it was mighty good to see him, to know that he was alive. Throughout this morning, whenever there was time for reflection, I found myself wondering about my close friends, wondering if they had been killed. Not wanting to inquire, I felt that their actual presence was the only trustworthy evidence that they were alive. After each explosion, the silent query: "Have more been killed? Who are they? I haven't seen Greene, Sheridan, Kasch, Catt, Berger, Morgan. Where is Fitz, and Bill Fox, and Red Harris?" After every explosion these questions clamored to be answered, and there were explosions almost every minute. It is more important to pray for them than to worry about them. I had already prayed for them as I had for all aboard, no more, no less. But emotionally there is special concern for personal friends, and even chaplains have emotions. Fortunately, the work at hand demanded attention almost constantly, and too insistent thoughts about friends were shut out. But the sight of Joe Taylor brought a sigh of relief: "Thank God. And keep him safe."

When I arrived on the flight deck, a quick visit once again to each of the wounded there gave assurance that, for the present, all had been done for them that could be done.

Thus far, my work had been with the wounded and the dying who were accessible on fo'c'sle or forward flight deck. Attendance on these latter had been interrupted a few times when a particularly bad explosion made it imperative that we search on the fringes of the fires and rescue victims of the blast. These we dragged and carried to the forward section to join the other patients. After such interruptions I resumed my individual sick calls, praying, absolving, anointing. Occasionally, also, I would be concerned about those who, although not physically wounded, were mentally stunned. "Gats" had already begun his extraordinarily good work in calming such boys, and I tried to copy him.

While concentrating on such specialized chaplain work, I had scarcely adverted to the great activity that went on about me. Now I noticed officers and men who from the first explosion had been working against prohibitive odds, taking desperate chances in their efforts to save the ship. I saw hose lines writhing and criss-crossing along the deck. Hose handlers crouch and fall in the blast of another explosion, then get to their feet and grip the hoses again. I saw the look of disgust when a line went dry as another water main ruptured. I saw them hunt for another main, link their hose, and start again in the battle against the fires. With few exceptions I recall no individual faces. It was a composite picture of bravery and devotion to duty of the surviving officers and men aboard the *Franklin*. But "Steamboat" Graham was there, the fire marshal; and Bill Hale was in general charge of the flight deck.

Despite the continued explosions of bombs and rockets, some progress against the fires had been made. Several hundred feet of the forward flight deck had been won from the flames, and the island structure was visible and occasionally accessible. But our speed had decreased to zero. We were dead in the water despite the valiant work of the engineers.

By devious telephone connection, communication was still possible between the bridge and the engineering department. The multiple intership communication network—"squawk boxes," direct-line telephones, general telephone circuits—had been put out of service by the explosions. But a few sound-power phones were still operating. Though the wires connecting even these emergency phones throughout the ship were for the most part blown out, the line connecting the engine room and the after-steering room had not parted, nor had the line connecting "Steering Aft" and bridge.

Trapped in this after-steering room were five boys. Holbrook Davis was there and Bill Hamel, Jim Gudbrandsen, Larry Costa, and Norman Mayer. At their battle stations when the first Jap bomb struck, they could have escaped from their compartment far below the water line, they could have climbed ladders up and aft to the fantail, and thence perhaps to safety. But it was their battle station. If the regular steering mechanism was disrupted, the guidance of the ship would devolve upon them with directions telephoned from the bridge. They stuck to their post. Then our own ammunition began to go off, above and about them. They heard the roar of explosions, the crash of ripped steel, the peculiar hiss of rockets tearing crazy paths through nearby compartments. They felt the heat of the adjacent fires that made their own compartment a furnace. They saw nothing; the lights had gone out and they were trapped in a hot dark tomb. They knew their chances of rescue were slim. But, meanwhile, they could relay messages from the captain to the engineers.

Engineers! My thoughts had turned to Tommy Greene, the chief engineer who at breakfast had been griping with me about the cold toast—oh, such a long time ago! With the first bomb he had vanished. Was he dead? Where had he gone? Tommy Greene was very much alive. At the crack of the first explosion Tommy was out of the wardroom. Heedless of smoke, flame, and battered bulkheads he made for the Engineer Control Office. The office had been wrecked by the Jap bomb. Hurrying forward and down another deck, nearer to the engines, Greene set up the engineering headquarters in the Warrant Officers' mess.

Division officers reported, orders were relayed to machinists, electricians, water tenders, and firemen. While racking explosions tore great chunks out of the ship, the engineers kept the steam up, kept the propellers turning. It was hot, and becoming hotter. Heavy acrid smoke penetrated these lower compartments. Men donned gas masks or rescue breathing equipment and stayed at their boilers and turbines and switch panels. Number Two fireroom, its uptakes blasted, the flame under the boilers snuffed out, was useless after the first explosion. At 8:30 Number One fireroom was out of commission. Officers and men concentrated their efforts on the after engine room and fireroom. Lieutenant Artz, Ensign Tucker, Ensign Haylor, Machinist Ensign, and their "Black Gang" crew could not hold out much longer. The explosions were ripping gashes in the steam lines. It was a losing fight to sustain pressure, and it was fast becoming a losing fight to sustain life as the thermometers cracked at temperatures of 200 degrees. Smoke had replaced air, and rescue breathers were spent. Tommy Greene couldn't keep his men at those stations much longer. Lieutenant Artz collapsed; Machinist's Mate Nott took charge of that plant. In the other plant, Haylor and Ensign hunted escape hatches for their men.

Through the medium of "Steering Control Aft" came a message to the bridge. "The engineers request permission, sir, to leave their stations. Commander Greene reports men are collapsing from heat and suffocation." From Captain

Gehres: "Permission granted. Tell the engineering officer before leaving to set the engines at eight knots if possible." Choked, agonized, the engineers climbed ladders and escape hatches.

A final word to Greene from forward engine: "Will someone with a breather come to forward engine room? We are trapped." Lieutenants White and Bostain rescued Nott, Artz, and two companions from the forward engine room. Machinist's Mate Baker set the controls at eight knots before abandoning the after engine room.

The firerooms aft were not yet abandoned. There it was still possible to live, and boilers had to be tended. Steam pressure must be kept up if at all possible. Barry and Reese stayed. They stayed almost beyond human endurance, and they left only when the boilers no longer functioned. In the bowels of a burning, exploding ship, in rooms where smoke blackened vision and choked lungs, they stayed with their crews until 9:30. At that time the boilers lost feed-water suction and were useless. Only then were the after firerooms abandoned. Barry and his men—Tony Godleski, Cliff Farmer, Jimmy Collum, Shorty Wilson, and Tiny Rials—managed to get up to the hangar deck, but they couldn't make their way forward through the fires on the deck and were forced to leap overboard. Reese, with McRae, Doll Buckner, and Jim Harris were able to work their way forward to the fo'c'sle.

At 9:30 in the morning steam stopped flowing from the boilers, turbines stopped generating power, screws stopped turning. Fifty miles offshore the *Franklin* lay dead in the water, drifting toward Japan.

CHAPTER SIX

Drifting Toward Japan

NOW IT was 9:30—only two and one-half hours since sunrise and the Jap bombs which came with it. Much had happened, many had died in those two and one-half hours. The *Franklin* was still ablaze, still exploding.

The cruiser *Santa Fe* approached from the starboard quarter. If she couldn't help a dead ship she might at least rescue dying men.

"Are your magazines flooded?" Captain Fitz yelled through a megaphone. An old-fashioned megaphone came in very handy when explosions had blasted all our supermodern electrical communication devices. The communication officer of the *Santa Fe* had been asking the same question over every radio frequency at his disposal. The message never reached us. Every receiving set of the *Franklin* had been put out of commission.

But the blast of Captain Fitz's voice rose above the din and confusion. He was thinking of the fate of the *Birmingham* when she went to assist the stricken *Princeton*. A mighty explosion on that carrier had inflicted horrible casualties aboard the assisting cruiser. "Are your magazines flooded?"

Back came the answer from Captain Gehres: "I have ordered them flooded, and believe they are." Every possible precaution had been taken.

In emergencies chances must be taken; not foolhardy chances, but calculated risks balanced against advantages. So the *Santa Fe* came alongside and tried to hold a course thirty feet off. She couldn't hold it. The *Franklin*, listing ever more dangerously, and dead in the water, veered at erratic angles away from the ship which proffered help. The operation had to be abandoned. Captain Fitz ordered lines cast off, and the *Santa Fe* departed, her mission unaccomplished.

This was an unhappy moment for our hundreds of seriously wounded men. It hurt to look into their eyes. Though they didn't say a word, they could not dissemble their disappointment as they saw the rescue ship depart. Their eyes reflected the horror of the immediate past and foresaw the despair of the immediate future.

His leg torn off, a makeshift tourniquet sopping with blood binding the stump, a boy lay in a stretcher on the flight deck. What chance had he now? At any moment the ship might capsize; at any moment the deck might blow up. If he lived through either or both of those perils, what then? In his stretcher he would float in the water just long enough to suffer a little longer, but not long enough for a destroyer to effect rescue. His only chance of survival seemed to lie in transfer by stretcher to the *Santa Fe*. And now the *Santa Fe* had gone. Hard straits even for the uninjured, but a legless cripple, weak from loss of blood, stunned by combat shock, helpless, what chance had such as he now? The boy said not a word, but in his eyes one read a bitter prophecy.

It was embarrassing to read so much in the eyes of a wounded boy. Yet I'm glad I noticed. Not much could be done for him, but the reassurance that he had not been abandoned by shipmates would ease his frightened heart.

"It's tough, lad, but keep your chin up; your buddies will stand by you no matter what happens. Never forget that. And say a prayer. That helps too, you know."

The wounded men who already had received medical and spiritual attention had been marshaled in the forward part of the ship. As I went aft in search of others who might need help, I passed the Number One elevator well. The enormous platform had been tipped askew at a forty-degree angle; its heavy steel pistons had bent like hairpins. Flames from the hangar deck fires leaped through the well, but not as viciously as before. To pass the spot was still dangerous, for foamite and oil from hot oakum smeared the deck. With any sudden lurch of the listing ship I might slip and fall through the well into the fires below.

The rapid increase of the list was alarming. I could almost see, and definitely could feel, the ship tipping more and more to starboard. If the list continued to increase at its present rate we would soon capsize.

With good fortune I passed the elevator well and approached the fire lines which at this time were about abreast of the island. The smoke was not so dense now, but the flames were as bad as ever. Lengths of hose sprawled along the deck from the forward section, near the wounded, to the fire lines here. Such a raging fire and so little hose presented a pathetic picture. What hose was available had to be coupled in many sections to reach from fire lines to forward mains, the only mains which had escaped destruction in the explosions.

The hose also lacked sufficient pressure. The vast engineering plant was dead, and the only source of power aboard was a small emergency Diesel engine. Al Collins had the job of starting and tending that Diesel whenever the ship was called to battle stations. He had started the engine early in the morning. He tended it all day.

Although the danger had not decreased, some order had emerged from the initial confusion. Organized fire fighting, starting at the forward flight deck and working aft, had been begun almost immediately after the bombing by those who were forward and topside. They were joined continually by others who had been able to work their way up from below decks.

Men in the stern were out of contact with the captain. Some on the after hangar deck had access only to the fantail. Their forward progress was blocked by white-hot fires, magnesium bombs glowing on the armor plate of the planes that had carried them. Men below on the second and third decks or climbing to the after hangar deck had been forced further aft. Dozens had been blown over the side. Others, enveloped by flames, had been forced to leap. For hours little groups struggled to get to the fantail, where they fought the fires with any means at their command until their position became unbearable. Then they too ditched into the sea.

Central Damage Control Station was located far below the main deck in a compartment near the keel of the ship. Shortly after the explosions began lights flashed red, signaling that fire had penetrated the main magazines. Lieutenant Billington and his crew expected momentarily the explosion which would tear the ship to pieces. All communications were out except those with the forward repair party. The men in C.D.C. were trapped incommunicado, watching that red eye flashing its fearful message. It was many tense hours before they discovered that the message was erroneous, owing to damaged wiring.

When the ship began to list badly and smoke poured into

the deck hold, Central Damage Control, with all communication lost, was abandoned. Chief Electrician Hoffner located an escape trunk which led up to the third deck, helped his men through, and then led them to the fo'c'sle to join the fire-fighting parties forward.

Some few, from topside, went below decks on special and very dangerous missions.

Gunners Stoops and Arlo Catt had gone down to flood the main magazines on order from the captain. These were gunners in charge of the ammunition. Hundreds of tons of explosives in the bowels of the ship must be covered with water. Stoops and Catt somehow managed to get to the flood valves. They turned them on and reported "Mission accomplished." It was not their fault, nor did anyone know until long afterward, that the valves controlled no water. The mains had ruptured. The ammunition in the forward magazines remained dry.

Many men fought fire amidships until their rescue breathers were exhausted, then made their way to the side of the hangar deck and dropped into the sea.

Shipfitter Burd had been in the after mess hall when the Jap bombs hit. He broke out a fire hose and wet three hundred rockets, rendering them harmless. Then he rounded up and led at least sixty men back to the fantail and escape. Burd went back for others and found himself amidships, trapped by new explosions aft and prevented by fire from going forward. He was forced to the side of the hangar and took to the sea. For five hours he floated on a raft with Chief Tony Hungaro, Dennis Koleh, and Shipfitter Kirkman. They were picked up by the carrier *Hornet*.

Many a man like Burd did his valiant deed before he was overwhelmed by the elemental forces of the catastrophe. The number of heroes will never be known.

Seaman Red Skelton, a gunner, and his buddy were standing side by side. An explosion blew his buddy to bits and catapulted Skelton into the water.

Lieutenant Fitzgerald of the engineers and dozens of men in separate groups made their way to the fantail, only to be forced off. Austin, Sheppard, Gregg, Batticki, Seaman Russo, Private Kane—their number will never be known.

Yeomen Brown and Cavello leaped into the water together. Cavello could not swim and had no life jacket. Brown gave him his. Brown was not rescued.

Sergeant Truax, with a handful of marines, had manned the guns on the fantail till fires forced them into the sea. Truax handed his life belt to a young lad who could not swim. Truax was not rescued.

On the forward flight deck the fire lines were abreast of the island by 9:30 A.M. From the bridge the captain supervised the fire fighting; on the deck Bill Hale was in general charge. Steamboat Graham, the fire marshal, was there with Davis, West, Berger, Harris, McKinney. Enlisted men were there too, working as hard and taking as desperate chances as their officers.

Bombs rolled about the deck, licked by flames to such heat they were painful to touch. Lieutenant Commander Stone, with helpers like Chief Orendorff, Bill Fowler, Boyd, and Jacobs rolled them over the side and into the sea.

Deeper in the fire line, Red Morgan was struggling singlehandedly with a hose, skidding on the slippery deck and vainly trying to do the work of six men.

"Don't you want some help, Red?"

"Hi, Pa-dre." Red had regained his drawl despite the excitement. In fact, Red wasn't excited. "I sure could use some help, if you could get me some men."

The strength of many young hands could accomplish more

than my feeble efforts, however willingly offered. I headed forward looking for help.

As I trudged along a lad spotted the cross on my helmet. He ran over to me, and asked in a not too steady voice, "Father, give me absolution." To the lad, whose name I do not even know, I explained that when the first bomb exploded I had given general absolution, then added, "Say an act of contrition and I'll give you absolution now."

He knelt on the listing flight deck. In the background flames shot high in the air, smoke billowed into the sky. Even during the short time it takes to say an act of contrition, there were explosions. The boy finished his prayer of sorrow for having offended God, and I concluded absolution. As he rose to his feet I recalled Red Morgan and his need of help.

"Look, lad, will you go down now to the fire lines and help Lieutenant Red Morgan with the hose?"

The boy looked me in the eyes, and with complete simplicity and sincerity said, "Sure, Father, I'll go anywhere now."

There it is: One doesn't necessarily need religious peace to fight a fire, but even for fighting a fire peace of soul helps. I began to realize then the power of the Cross, the white cross painted on my helmet, a power of recognition and of inspiration.

The fury, the flames, and the smoke had made inspiration essential and recognition almost impossible. Flames had seared flesh, and smoke had smeared faces. It was difficult to identify anyone in the ship. The men could not recognize officers not attached to their own division. The fury of initial explosions had paralyzed men's minds. When the explosions began to subside, minds began to function. The men were looking for a sign. Trained to obey at a sign from division officer or chief, the men could find neither. Divisions were disorganized; key officers had been killed, Chiefs were dispersed or trapped or dead. But the men could recognize the chaplain. Despite the fury, the smoke, they could recognize the sign of the Cross on his helmet.

The power of the Cross to inspire surpassed its power of recognition. "Sure, Father, I'll go anywhere now." That was the simple reaction of a boy who felt the influence of the Cross. Boys of all faiths would go anywhere if the chaplain would go with them.

In turn I had to shoulder my cross, however unpleasant, however dangerous. I had to go with my boys wherever they were needed. My source of strength? The same power of the Cross.

I asked eight men to come with me and help Commander Hale, Lieutenant Harris, and Lieutenant Morgan. Eight men came to the fire lines, then another eight, and another. When one hose crew, choking with smoke, had reached the limit of endurance, another crew would relieve it.

The men were not following me as much as they were following the Cross. For better or worse, I had become a symbol. My helmet was far more important than my head.

In turn, the helmet protected my head not only with physical protection from shrapnel, but with spiritual protection from shock at the prospect of death. Before many minutes or many seconds I might be blown to bits. That really didn't matter provided I were blown to the real "kingdom come." Meanwhile, the men should try to save the ship and rescue trapped shipmates. With the power of the Cross I could help them.

Up on the bridge Commander Steve Jurika, the navigator, no longer navigated. We were dead in the water, drifting toward Japan. But he was keeping the log. That also was part of his job. It is a marvel to me that under extraordinary tension Steve could confine himself to writing that rigid data, prose from which every drop of pathos had been eliminated. He squeezed out the heroism and wrote down the so-called facts. That was his job. He was assigned to write the log. The navigator does not tell the truth; he merely reports the scientifically verifiable. Later on in this tale, the reader will find that Steve had a soft and wounded heart. He and I both had near relatives in the Philippines.

This is Steve's log, and in its deadpan notations we can read a concise, if colorless, catalogue of the events of that wild morning.

0657 commenced launching aircraft of strike 2B. 0708 ship under attack by enemy aircraft. Took two bomb hits, first bomb hit flight deck frame 68, exploded hangar deck frame 82; second bomb hit flight deck frame 133, exploded frame 142. 0709 general quarters. 0712 set condition Zebra. At the time of the attack 36 VF and 9 VB were airborne. 0725 (about) ship steadied on 355 (t). 0800 Rear Admiral R. Davison and staff were transferred to U.S.S. *Miller* (DD535). 0815 assumed starboard list 3 degrees. Fires and explosions occurring throughout the ship. 0840 starboard list increased to 6 degrees. 0931 *Santa Fe* approached and lay to about 100 feet off starboard bow to remove wounded. 0945 lost steering control and all communications except to steering aft from bridge. Set all engines ahead 8 knots and abandoned engine rooms due to smoke and heat. 0952 after 5"/38 magazines exploded. 1000 starboard list steadied at 13 degrees. Ship dead in water. 1015 *Santa Fe* backed off snapping all lines. 1050 *Santa Fe* alongside for second time. All wounded and unnecessary personnel were removed. 1225 *Santa Fe* cleared ship. 1254 Japanese Judy made glide bombing attack, bomb missing starboard side of ship. 1404 *Franklin* taken under tow by U.S.S. *Pittsburgh* on southerly course at 2 knots. Ships present include 3 screening destroyers, *Pittsburgh,* and *Santa Fe.* 1505 *Franklin* headed 180 (t) at 6 knots under tow.

At 0952 (Steve told me the exact time much later) the most terrific blast of all occurred. A five-inch ready service magazine blew up. The ship felt like a rat being shaken by an angry cat. Whole aircraft engines with propellers attached, debris of all description, including pieces of human bodies, hurtled into the air and then descended like hail upon a roof.

It was a fierce explosion, and I don't know how we survived it. Knocked from our feet, we remained on the decks, each one instinctively "crawling into his helmet." Even if we survived the explosion, how could we escape the falling shrapnel? That hail of debris lasted for many seconds, and thoughts are swift in such seconds. I do not think I was afraid of death then, although I did realize the chances were great.

Christ said that for his followers death is the gateway to heaven. All my life I had been trained to take Christ's teachings at face value. From this viewpoint death did not seem fearful.

But the boys! They were youngsters; their lives were before them; they did not want to die. I felt a special responsibility for those whom I had asked to help at the fire lines. If they hadn't followed me, they would have been forward in the ship, far from the explosion.

"Please, God, spare them!" Aspirations come swiftly to a chaplain sprawled on a deck as shrapnel is hurtling down on all sides.

But at length the storm was over. The hail of debris grew lighter and then stopped. We rose to our feet. Immediately the hoses were manned again by all the boys—all except two. Two bodies lay motionless, lapped by flames. Ready hands helped and the two were carried forward to where the wounded lay. I administered the sacraments, the last rites.

But the boys were not dead. God had been good to us. The explosion of the magazine where the five-inch shells were stored might well have sent the ship to its death and all the men with her. But no one was killed by this explosion, even though the boys at the fire lines had been working in the very heart of danger. The two who were wounded by the blast, knocked unconscious and momentarily threatened by flames and suffocation, had not been seriously hurt. It could have been the protection of the Cross.

God also sent protection for the wounded. The *Santa Fe* came in again. When Captain Fitz had ordered lines cast off, he had not forgotten our wounded. He had left only to maneuver, the better to effect rescue. She had swung in a big circle, and now the *Santa Fe* came at us again. Out of the smoke-hidden starboard quarter she came plowing toward us at incredible speed.

"She's coming fast," someone yelled.

"She's *got* to come fast," Captain Gehres answered aloud to himself.

Close alongside, at a speed of twenty-two knots, she tore through our horizontal radio masts, tore through the over-hanging debris of still hot steel, crunched through our projecting gun platforms and our outboard catwalks. The impact sheared her own decks.

At twenty-two knots she plowed through the entanglements and obstructions which at slower speed would have been a trap for her. Hull grinding against hull, the bows of the two ships came into parallel line.

"Full speed astern. Cast over the lines!" The rescue ship was moored to the burning wreck.

"Ahoy, *Franklin!* Send over your wounded."

Captain Gehres summarized the spectacle: "The greatest piece of seamanship I have ever seen."

By makeshift mailbag breeches buoys, the stretcher cases were lifted to safety. Across a narrow plank with a single guide line, volunteers carried their wounded buddies to the *Santa Fe*.

This transfer of wounded had to be executed with care and speed, a difficult combination. Transfer to the safety of the *Santa Fe* would not help a dying boy if careless handling caused fatal aggravation of wounds. But too careful transfer at the expense of speed could be fatal both to the boy and to the *Santa Fe*.

We were in a precarious position. Two ships were locked together, and one fiercely blazing and threatening more explosions, a constant threat to herself and her helper. Moreover, both ships were immobile, "sitting ducks," an easy target for the enemy.

Jap planes were again approaching the formation. We had had alarms but as yet no attacks. However, we were only fifty miles offshore. From their airfields, planes could fly out in fifteen minutes. The pilots need not even take time to plot a course. Our pillar of smoke was a guiding cloud.

As yet no Jap had penetrated the combat air patrol which our sister carriers had supplied when we were hit. But they would continue their assaults, and eventually some would get through. If the *Santa Fe* were alongside when that attack came against us, both ships could be destroyed. The transfer of the wounded from *Franklin* to *Santa Fe* had to be executed with speed.

But traffic between the two ships was not just one-way. While up forward the wounded from the *Franklin* were carried to the cruiser, Captain Fitz's fire fighters manned all hoses, and were pouring tons of water into our after hangar deck, fighting fires which we could not yet reach. As they pushed the flames back, the boys of the *Santa Fe* came forward and leaped or climbed aboard the *Franklin,* dragging hoses with them. Throughout the long period the *Santa Fe* was alongside, some were aboard the *Franklin* in the thick of the fires. Stout ship, the *Santa Fe!*

This was no time for idle admiration. From the fo'c'sle the hazardous and tricky process of transferring wounded went on under the direction of Commander Joe Taylor, with Commander Doc Smith, Lieutenant Commander Downes, Chaplain Gatlin, and many others assisting. On the flight deck, just as hazardously, the transfer continued in a double line with Commander Bill Hale in general charge and Kilpatrick, the fighter pilot, masterfully supervising the operation of the breeches buoy. Sam Sherman was there with a word of encouragement for the desperately wounded and a final administration of first aid.

Transfer of the wounded brought temporary cessation to my amateur fire-fighting activities. Once more I saw each of the boys. Their appreciation of little efforts to help them and to soothe them brought tears to my eyes. A prayer, or a light word of banter. Pat a lad on the shoulder or tuck in the blanket, and his soul looks out at you through his eyes.

If a lad was well enough to talk, he would quickly tell you not to waste time on him—his buddy in the next stretcher needed help.

"Look, he's bleeding and I think he's unconscious; put him ahead of me. Let him go across first." Shipmates are like that.

Captain Gehres from his position on the bridge surveyed all the destruction and the activity. Nothing escaped him. Looking aft he saw gasoline spewing from a vent, cascading to the sea in liquid flames. Looking forward at the catwalk between the two lines of wounded he saw more liquid spouting. If it caught fire the wounded would be helplessly trapped.

"Padre," he shouted down at me, "for God's sake find out if that's gasoline. If it is, get the wounded away from there fast!"

"I don't see where you mean, Captain. I'll go up the deck and you direct me by signals."

I walked up the slippery, sloping deck. The journey offered several seconds for careful thought. How will I tell whether the stuff is gasoline? I'll have to taste it. The human mind develops peculiar kinks; I wasn't thinking serious thoughts. My mind by some quirk fastened on one fixed idea: "If this is gasoline, and I taste it, and it catches fire, I'll sure look silly. What a time to practice fire eating!"

Captain Gehres was pointing down and outboard. I saw the spurting liquid. Bending down I lifted cupped hands to my lips. Salt water never tasted so delicious! The geyser came from a burst main, close by a gasoline outlet. Thumbs up to the captain! "O.K., no danger from this source."

But I still felt silly. I had to explain to someone that my actions were not as foolish as they might appear. I explained it to Lieutenant W. A. Simon, who happened to be nearby. It gave him momentary respite from the ordeal he had suffered.

Simon's battle station was the Combat Information Center. It is the nerve center of combat operations, a double compartment situated between the flight and hangar decks, in the gallery deck. An explosion had burst directly below, thrusting the deck floor upward, hurling all hands against the steel overhead. Simon alone escaped; how, he will never know. In the adjacent ready room, where a few pilots of Kilpatrick's squadron were on duty, none escaped.

Kilpatrick himself was just now supervising the transfer of the last of the wounded. An order was passed by word of mouth that all air-group personnel would now cross over to the *Santa Fe*. Their job is flying, not fire fighting.

Commander Hale communicated the captain's orders. But Kilpatrick is a stubborn Scotsman.

"I'll stay aboard here and help out."

"You'll do what you're told! Get across to the *Santa Fe* and take your pilots with you."

Orders that connote safety to themselves are disagreeable to brave men when danger threatens others. But orders are orders. Kilpatrick crossed to the cruiser.

Doc Sherman was attached to the air group, and hence had orders to leave. But Sam's case was somewhat different, and with a deep sense of duty he realized it.

"Captain, I can't leave this ship. I'm a doctor and you need doctors. There are no more wounded now, but there may be later."

"Sam, you're attached to the air group and you may go with them if you wish. But we do need doctors."

Sam stayed aboard the *Franklin*.

The evacuation of the wounded completed, my thoughts returned to the fire fighters, to the officers and men who through the long process of transferring stretchers had continued their efforts steadfastly against desperate odds.

Starting toward the fire line along the starboard side I came upon a scene that looked even more fantastic than my "fire-eating" episode. Gerald Smith, Fireman 1st Class from Oswego, New York, was practicing acrobatics! Ankles held by two shipmates, he dangled head down over the deck edge, hanging in space between the two ships. Shifting on the swells of the open sea, the *Santa Fe* kept banging against our projecting gun mounts. In an erratic swell the gun mounts could be smashed to bits, and then so would Smitty's head.

"Smitty, there are pleasanter ways to commit suicide. What are you doing?"

Smitty couldn't answer, but his buddies explained. As the cruiser came alongside, she cut one of our hose lines. Smitty was replacing it, despite the danger to himself. There were few enough water mains which were serviceable. We couldn't afford to abandon the one to which this hose was attached.

Not infrequently during this period, I became a messenger on the flight deck. The cross on my helmet was readily recognized by the captain on the bridge. Whenever he had to send a message it was easy for him to identify me and attract my attention.

"Padre, get the engineers together. We must keep them a unit. Spread the word to the engineering officers."

I struggled up and down the listing deck.

"Engineers, engineers, are there any engineers? Officers or petty officers?"

I felt like a peddler. No peddler amid the hurly-burly of the market place ever hawked his wares with such stridence and such insistence as I called for engineers amid the bedlam of the flight deck.

When the engineers had abandoned stations, many were unable to reach the fo'c'sle and were forced to leap into the sea. Others had the luck to choose passages and escape hatches which enabled them eventually to climb topside in the forward section of the ship. From their engineering posts where they had been enduring temperatures above the 200 mark, and had been blinded and choked with smoke, these officers and men came topside to suffer the cutting chill of the open sea.

They saw for the first time the havoc which had been

wrought upon the ship; they saw fires which were still raging. Water tenders became hose tenders, firemen became firemen of a different kind. It was necessary that these engineers be kept organized as a unit. If ever the flames were put under control, then the engineers could perhaps repair our power plant and give us steerage. Otherwise, our work was quite in vain. We were drifting toward Japan.

"Engineers, are there any engineers here?" I trudged along the flight deck peddling my wares. In not too long a time the engineering department was organized by divisions, although each division had but a small fraction of its usual complement. Throughout the day these men helped against the flames, but they were ready to resume their engineering duties as soon as the heat abated below.

Captain Gehres was alert even for details. Long after the engine rooms had cooled sufficiently to make occupancy safe, the heavy smoke would remain. He knew rescue breathers would be needed. He asked the *Santa Fe* to give us some of theirs, and directed Graham, the fire marshal, to forage for more in Damage Control Eight, aft of the island, where no one yet had penetrated since the first mighty explosions.

Graham went back to investigate. If rescue breathers stored in Damage Control Eight had survived the explosions they might be salvaged now before the fires consumed them. The need of the breathers justified the risk. But Graham didn't seem even to be aware of the risk. He strolled aft, and was lost in the thick smoke.

I didn't want to go into that choking smoke that concealed the deck, and perhaps concealed a hole where the deck had been. The trip led toward the hottest of fires, raging around an ammunition turret. I didn't want to go, but I didn't want to let Steamship Graham go alone. He didn't seem to have sense enough to appreciate the danger. Perhaps he was in a walking daze and needed me to talk some sense into him. So I went after him.

The smoke was less thick aft. It was easy to see Danger Control Eight had long since disintegrated. Graham's trek was fruitless, but it was brave nonetheless.

Captain Fitz gave us some rescue breathers which we stored in a place we hoped was safe. If we could ever get back to the firerooms and get the turbines turning, those rescue breathers would shorten our "sitting duck" period by hours.

From the *Santa Fe* we also got bread, a big bag of it, all they had ready baked. To turn attention from the perilous and heroic drama of the *Franklin* to thoughts of food was rankest bathos. But if the captain made good his bold decision, "We can save this ship," then we would need the bread. Eventually, though it seemed far off now, danger might lessen and heroism give way to hunger. No food was accessible on the *Franklin*.

The *Santa Fe* had accomplished her task and accomplished it supremely well. She must cast off her lines now and leave us to fate. No, not fate, but Providence! We had Faith. But however steadfast our Faith, for a moment we turned wistful, almost envious eyes to the departing *Santa Fe*. For better or worse, listing badly, still blazing fiercely, dead in the water, now forty-five miles from Japan, and drifting closer, we were alone.

CHAPTER SEVEN

Afternoon, March 19, 1945

THOUGH THE *Santa Fe* left her place alongside, she didn't desert us. It was good to see her circling some two thousand yards away, guarding us against the Jap planes that appeared again and again, anxious to get in the death blow. As the *Santa Fe* stood guard, her sister ship, the *Pittsburgh,* took over. Hers was the task of getting under tow this burning hulk that was the *Franklin,* the ship that refused to sink. Captain Gehres detailed Joe Taylor, his executive officer, to handle the *Franklin* end of the towing business. Joe said, "Aye, aye, sir," which interpreted meant, "Captain, can't you think of some easier feat of seamanship?"

How does one go about getting a towline on a 27,000-ton ship, blazing, and dead in the water, with no power, no winches, nothing but the will to do what seemed impossible? It involved hauling a quarter-mile of six-inch steel cable, dragging it by hand, by muscles of back and arms. A thousand able-bodied men might be able to do it, but the *Franklin* didn't have a thousand able-bodied men. Available aboard were some 350 men, and of these only about eighty could be spared to haul the towline. A quarter of a mile of six-inch steel cable: eighty men couldn't budge it—and they didn't. Joe Taylor drove them, "Heave ho, heave ho!" Strive as they might—boatswains, machinists, seamen, stewards, black and white lined up shoulder to shoulder. Officers and men sweating and straining—the towline didn't move an inch.

Then something happened. Uncertainly, and slowly at first, but gathering volume until they overcame the roar of flames, the Negro boys under the leadership of Frasure, Steward'smate 1/C, started an impromptu chanting, making up the words as they went along, with the refrain coming in a crescendo chorus, "Heave ho, heave ho." It was a Negro spiritual created on the fo'c'sle of a dying ship; and as the rhythm of their voices found certainty, the rhythm of the gang's muscles and sinews started to have its effect. The heavy towline began to move. How, God only knows; but it was certainly the Negro stewards who supplied the emotional impetus for a superhuman job.

But, however superhuman and heroic the task of hauling a long steel cable, the process of getting under tow a ship the size of the *Franklin* still isn't quite as simple as that. It's a complex job, and its success depends upon coordination between the ship towing and the ship being towed. Hence a need for quick communication between the two. While the gang was hauling the towline, a radioman was at work on the flight deck improvising a portable radio, setting up a short-wave set for communication with the *Pittsburgh*. To him the explosions which constantly threatened death were nuisances and nothing more. Radiomen, from the early days of the breed, have been notorious "bugs," and Stone was a perfect specimen of the class. Nothing could divert him from tinkering with his "homemade" set. Despite fire, explosions, smoke and listing ship he had radio contact with the *Pittsburgh* within an hour.

While Stone may have been distracted by his absorption in radio, the rest of us felt the full impact of a new danger. We discovered there on the flight deck, within forty feet of the radioman, a live-fused unexploded bomb, one of the many thousand-pounders. What to do? How could we keep it horizontal despite the slippery, listing deck? Lieutenant Graham and Lieutenant Commander George Stone worked on the fuse while five boys held the hot bomb horizontal, since a sudden lurch would have detonated the head.

Quite by chance, I was present when the bomb was discovered. I couldn't do much. I didn't know how. But there is such a thing as moral support. So while others tinkered with the fuse or held the bomb steady, I stood by with what nonchalance I could assume. Very humbly I protest that this was not a mere pose. Hands and skill were needed; it was dangerous work and everyone knew it. At least I could stand by and participate in the danger—not for the sake of participating but as a means of telling the lads I wanted to be with them whenever they were in danger.

"Padre, we think the bomb is defused, but the mechanism is jammed and we can't be sure. If we keep it horizontal it can't explode whether armed or not; but when we drop it overboard the head will turn down and it might explode while falling. Will you get the boys off the fo'c'sle? If this thing does go off they might get killed down there."

There is a thwartship catwalk over the fo'c'sle, a natural setting for a balcony speech. But what a speech! Above the din I shouted:

"Is there any officer here? Who is the officer in charge?"

Lieutenant Commander Downes identified himself and stood by. As I looked down I could see most of the men busy at the towline. There were some there, however, who for the moment were not occupied. "Boys, if you're working here, then keep working; if you're not working, come topside to the flight deck. We're throwing a bomb overboard and it might explode as it passes the fo'c'sle. If you're not working here don't stay here. If you are working keep at it; you have to take the chance."

Just another hazard the towline gang had to contend with! But the bomb disposal officers had done their job well, and the bomb was safely jettisoned.

It may seem surprising that there was anyone on the fo'c'sle, anyone on the ship, for that matter, who was not occupied. I confess it seemed surprising to me at the time. Fortunately, before I could speak out of turn, I was given the facts by Chaplain Gatlin and Doc Fuelling.

"Hi, Jim, good to see you. I didn't see you about and I was afraid to ask."

"Padre, you almost didn't see me."

Then as the boys mounted the ladder from the fo'c'sle to the flight deck, Doc Fuelling told me of their adventure, gave me the explanation of the stunned, lackluster eyes I had noticed. These were the men who had been trapped in the after mess. compartment. Gary had left them with the hopeful promise: "I'll find a way out and I'll be back to lead you out. Do you hear me? I'll be back."

The mess where the several hundred men were trapped was on the Number 3 deck aft. Without lights it had become a black hole of heat and terror, for there were no portholes in the compartment. It was below the waterline. Gary's reassurance had heartened them, but the effect of his promise was soon dissipated in the mounting tension which communicated itself swiftly in a sightless dark that rocked and shuddered under repeated explosions. Why didn't he return?

None there knew the ship as Gary in his job as engineer

knew it. None of them realized their predicament. It was well they did not; their terror might easily have split open to its ugly core of panic.

A rapid, groping search told Don Gary that every exit was sealed off except one, and that led to a dead end in a bomb-storage compartment. He realized that in the heat and lurch of these insane moments the bombs might easily explode; but it was the only chance he had to get the men out alive, for the bomb-storage room led to a ventilator trunk. He removed the grate, shoved his thin body through the opening, and went back to the mess to keep his promise.

"Form a chain; each man grab another. Form a chain of twenty. The first man grab hold of me. I'll be back for the rest." And up the shaft the first twenty went, singly but swiftly. The confined ventilator ducts were choked with smoke. The possibility of asphyxiation was acute.

Gary knew the air-duct system thoroughly, but explosions had burst many of the ducts, and had sealed off others. Without knowledge of the progress and extent of the destruction to the ship, he could not be sure that a pipe he had chosen would not lead him to fire and another trap. He could choose his passage only by groping into the blackness and trying as much as possible to stay in the cooler, fresher ventilators in the hope that they would issue into a relatively safe deck area. His problem, as we look at it now after the event, can be simply stated: He had to find an undamaged sequence of pipes which would allow the men to crawl to safety from the mess on Number 3 deck, along the length of the ship for about two hundred yards, to the forward part of 01 deck, *six* decks above! When we put Gary's task back in its context of terror and urgency, we receive some idea of the heroism of the man, feeling his way starboard, port, forward, aft, up and down, improvising and revising his route each trip as fresh explosions sealed off new pipes. And he did go back. As each little group of twenty tumbled out into the open air, Gary stood by the ventilator. As soon as the last man wriggled free, Gary hoisted himself into the vent again. Down he went, and crawled along a twisting, devious burrow of smoke and fear, back to the trapped men in the after mess—a number of times—until every one of several hundred had been led to safety.

Jim didn't mention this fact to me, but the last to leave in the last group was Doc Jim Fuelling.

Others had made their own escapes from other below-deck compartments. Young Julius Payak, Pfc. in the Marine Corps from Portage, Pennsylvania, was brushing his teeth when the first bomb exploded: "When I looked up, the mirror in front of me was gone, and I decided it was time for me to go too. I ran into the Marine compartment just about seventy-five feet from where the bomb had hit. The smoke was starting to get me. My bunk was nearby, and it occurred to me that there should be some air in the mattress; I tore off the cover and buried my nose in it. Then I began crawling across the deck to the passage, and finally made it to the ammunition transfer room where it was possible to get some air because the uptakes were open. When I got my wind, I came topside." That was how Payak made his escape, and when he arrived on the flight deck he joined the fire fighters.

Another Marine private, Stephen Nowak, helped himself and a dozen others through suffocating smoke-filled compartments to a hatch which he forced open and through which he led his buddies to safety. At the foot of the ladder lay a sailor, asphyxiated, unconscious. That lad owed his life to Nowak, who carried him to safety.

As I stood on the thwartship platform, I didn't know the details of many of these escape stories. I knew only what

Jim Fuelling had told me about his group. But his story had solved a problem for me. Now I would not be unjustly condemning boys for what appeared to me to be failure to cooperate. There were many who listened but did not hear, who looked you in the eye but did not see. They were conscious but they didn't know it. They were for the time stunned, their lungs sucking in fresh air and more fresh air, now so plentiful, so free, but a short time ago so unobtainable. Later these boys would help, but for the moment their systems had to become readjusted to the mere fact of being alive.

Having been made aware that there were many on the fo'c'sle and forward flight deck who were incapable of helping, it was easier thereafter to pick out those men who were ready and able. You could tell by their eyes. Their eyes showed they understood what was said; before their feet took one step to follow, their eyes showed willingness to follow.

Heroic willingness was called for to accomplish a task which now challenged us. Lieutenant Commander William R. McKinney was the gunnery officer. From the first explosion he had been fighting fires; but he had another concern more pressing and more vital. He manned the hoses, pushing back the flames as a preliminary to this, his chief concern: to make accessible the forward gun turret and ready-ammunition magazine where hundreds of rounds of five-inch shells were stored. A similar turret aft had already blown up, the most terrific explosion in a day of terrific explosions. If the forward turret went off, the ship might be blown apart. Hundreds of lives would be saved if the ready ammunition could be dumped. But "Mac" couldn't dump the stuff alone, nor could he do it with only the help of Gunner Stoops and Ensign McCrary, who were working with their chief in what was peculiarly a gunnery department job. They needed volunteers to form a shell brigade, a chain of men to pass the hot shells from hand to hand from the inmost turret to the outboard catwalk where they could be dumped into the sea. A risky business.

Though I can truthfully say that by this time routine, and perhaps the momentary meditations on eternity I had been making all morning, had combined to remove all fear of danger to myself, it was quite another thing to ask others to join in assisting "Mac." I had here the heaviest kind of responsibility, responsibility for the lives of others. I said a quick prayer for the right decision and strength to follow it, one of the few moments in the day when I found time for explicit prayer for guidance.

As I went among the boys, I began to realize the weight of the responsibility for all the lives aboard which rested on Captain Gehres's shoulders. His ability to evaluate all factors and then make a decision and stand by it unless other factors appeared to change the situation, his strength of character, his willingness to assume great responsibility firmly, calmly and confidently, influenced my own behavior. With a prayer for guidance and with the skipper for example, I spoke to the boys: "Kids, Commander McKinney is dumping ammunition, five-inch shells; and they're hot. It's dangerous, but it's necessary. He needs help. Will you come?" More were willing than were needed. So our shell brigade joined McKinney, McCrary, and Stoops.

It's a queer sensation, pushing through smoke and flame to enter a turret filled with ammunition. The actual dangers didn't cause me much worry, but I have always been a victim of claustrophobia. For me to enter a small closed space such as that turret demands effort of the will, and it is accomplished only at the cost of cold sweat. I did not so much mind the thought of being blown up. I did very much mind being hemmed in. A silly phobia, I realized, but I confess it took an effort to overcome it.

Once in the turret, the men went quickly to work. A chain was formed to pass the ammunition. One of the boys caught the thought (pure Americana, and only Americans, I think, can act this way) and he called out: "Here it is, Padre. Praise the Lord and *dump* the ammunition." You can't beat kids with that spirit. They knew the danger, they felt the blisters forming on their fingers—the shells were that hot; they knew the shell they now held, or the one they were about to handle, or the next, or any one of the hundreds they were passing along the line might blow up in their faces. They knew that, but they had sense enough not to dwell on it. "Praise the Lord and dump the ammunition."

Fortunately, the boys didn't expect me to stay working in the line too long. One with creaking bones such as mine would slow up the operation. I do think, however, that they did want me to start off. You shouldn't ask lads to do what you yourself are not willing to do. However, despite creaking bones, I have no recollection that the shells felt heavy. I well remember they felt hot. Many days later, impelled by curiosity, I lifted a five-inch 38 shell. I could do it, but with difficulty, and slowly.

The boys were husky and didn't mind the weight of the shells. They didn't mind the danger either; from the beginning of the episode they had accepted it. But the heat and the smoke sapped their strength, and there soon was need of more volunteers.

The need was promptly met. A new shift was formed. It was only a matter of minutes to organize them, and they took over. But Mac stayed on; as gunnery officer he felt a special responsibility—he wasn't going to have his ammunition destroy the ship. This episode in the turret was difficult. I stayed with whatever gang was working within, and by the time the last bomb was jettisoned my brain and lungs were in need of air.

There were more shells on the deck below, many more than could be dumped in the time available. Besides, these were located in a magazine much more inaccessible than the turret—inaccessible, that is, to the men, but not to the flames. While the shell brigade dumped ammunition from the turret on the deck above, a hose crew worked its way through the smoke and fire until they reached the aperture of the magazine on the gallery deck. This space was confining too, and hence uncomfortable for a claustrophobe. But the ammunition was successfully flooded.

I realize that this account would be more valuable as history, and would present a clearer picture to the reader, if the events were chronologically catalogued. Commander Steve Jurika, the navigator who could not navigate a dead ship, kept an accurate log; that was one of his duties. But no one else aboard had any correct, adequate idea of the passage of time. There were periods of an hour's duration when, as for Joshua, the sun stood still. There were lapses of a minute which seemed extended over hours. Einstein has written learned treatises on the relativity of time, and many have followed him. Only Heidegger, to my knowledge, has adequately described the relativity of psychological time. On the *Franklin* on March 19th everyone except Steve Jurika was living psychological time. To a reader it would seem fantastic to say "three hours after a minute ago" or "a minute after three hours ago." For those on the *Franklin* it was not fantastic, it was actual—their only measure was psychological time. But it will be better to prescind from psychology, and say merely "some time later" or "about this time."

So, by this time, the fires on the flight deck had been pushed back to a point abreast the island, about midships. We were making progress, but it was slow, and the episode of the five-inch ready magazine had convinced Lieutenant "Steamboat" Graham that it wasn't sufficient to contend with the fires only on the flight deck. Immediately below was the gallery deck, and though we had successfully accomplished the flooding of the magazine, large quantities of other inflammable equipment were stored there. To be successful we'd have to fight the fire from the hangar deck as well as from above. Until now the hangar deck had been a blazing inferno into which no one could venture. But so intense had been the fire that anything there that could burn must long since have been consumed. Graham was determined to investigate. If heat and smoke were not too intense, a hose might be manned and the fires on the gallery deck attacked from below.

For the second time that morning I followed Graham, not because I wanted to, but because I thought he shouldn't go alone. Graham stood before the small door at the port-side catwalk in the gallery passageway directly beneath the flight deck. He hesitated but briefly. There was nothing unusual about this particular opening. Almost everywhere else bombs and rockets had torn openings through the sides of the ship; great holes with jagged edges which were frightening principally because no human plan had designed them. But the opening Graham began to enter was not frightening; it was a doorway in proper place and shape, as marked on the ship blueprints. But only empty darkness was inside, solid darkness which could hide the fact that the passage floors had been blown away, opaque darkness which no flashlight could dissipate.

"Are you going in?" I asked him.

"Yes."

"Then I'll follow. Go ahead."

"Crawl close after me on hands and knees. Use your light for what help it is. It won't help much; we'll have to feel our way. Don't push me, but keep close."

Graham wasn't afraid of the passage, but he didn't like it. Upon entering, he liked it less. Even with a companion at his heels, the dark uncertainty still pressed upon him from in front. The flight deck was bad, but it was open. You could see the flames and see your shipmates. In this passage the devil himself could be hiding and you couldn't see him. You couldn't even smell the devil here. Can't smell anything. Thick smoke stifles the instinct even before it stifles the lungs. Cough and spit it out and hope the residue has some air for breath of life. Can you hear the devil in this dark passage? You can hear a cacophony of noises which are devilish enough. Constant crackle of flames, near or distant; a noise compounded of whine and hiss and shriek followed by a muffled blast: another rocket! And water dripping, the sound of water trickling from the flight deck where it could help control flames and seeking the lower holds where it would try to capsize us.

Could you recognize the devil here even if you touched him, stumbling upon him with your hand poking forward into the blackness? Dank unknown things you did touch, or they touched you, eerie rotten debris lying on the deck or hanging along the walls. You crawled over it, passed bumping it. Whether or not Steamboat imagined the devil ahead, I think he appreciated that the Padre was at his heels.

Graham's crawl became slower, stopped. I drew abreast. We couldn't quite see: we felt empty space ahead. A hole in the deck showed faintly, slightly less black than the passage. Vague shapes, jagged steel stalactites hung down to a lower level. But the hole in the deck was not too big. Lying on the deck and holding to some projection, Graham swung his foot across the gap and tested for strength. Crawling and clinging to the sides, he was over. The passage ahead was darker, the smoke more choking. We had only been in the passage one hundred seconds, but they were very slow seconds; we had progressed only twenty feet down the passageway, but they were very long feet.

The hangar deck was hot, but not too filled with smoke, and there were no great fires. From here a hose crew could work on the gallery fires, provided the men were relieved about every twenty minutes. We returned for help.

On the second trip from topside we led a group of hose crew volunteers; but when we arrived below they were no longer with us. It wasn't like the boys to volunteer for hazardous duty and then call it quits. There must be some special explanation. There was. On the way down at a point where the smoke was thickest, Graham and I had crawled over a body, and failed to see it. Though fearless of death, the boys had an overwhelming awe for the dead! Again I said the prayers for a departed soul, and we moved the body. Then we led the hose crew down to the hangar deck, and valiantly they went to work.

While fires were being fought on hangar and flight decks, and shells dumped from blazing turrets, the *Franklin* was still a fighting ship and under continuous threat of air attack by the enemy. We didn't have many guns in working condition, but those we had must be manned. Most of the original gun crews had been killed in the initial blasts, and now a volunteer crew was organized to man the forty-millimeter mount above the bridge. Robert Oxley was a Gunner's Mate Third Class. He volunteered, as did Bob Dixon, Staff Sergeant, Marine Corps. Then there was Wilfred

Williams, third class yeoman; Charles Finkenster, who worked in the laundry; Wells Wilson and Audred Deliver, ordinary seamen.

As the motley group assembled, Wallace Klimkiewicz was standing by on the bridge. He had been on duty as the captain's orderly when we were hit, and there he had stayed. He most emphatically had stayed. When the explosions were at their height and the bridge was the most dangerous place on the ship, the captain told Klim to make his way forward to the fo'c'sle where it was safer. The captain is still chuckling at the answer.

"Begging the captain's pardon, sir, the captain's orderly will stay at his post."

Klim had held his post on the bridge until now, when a post of equal danger was open. He stepped up to the skipper.

"Begging the captain's pardon, sir, the captain's orderly requests permission to join the gun crew."

"But Klim, can you handle a forty-millimeter gun?"

"Captain, sir, a Marine can do anything!"

It was no idle boast. At least once, that gun crew was solely responsible for saving the ship. A Jap plane broke through our escort guard and made a bomb dive at us. These boys got a bead on the plane and forced the Jap to pull out of his dive just enough to throw the bomb some fifty feet astern. The Jap missed because they made him miss!

That near miss was a relief to those of us above decks, but it was one more torture of the unknown to the boys trapped in steering aft. These were the boys who had relayed messages from the bridge to the engineers, boys who from the first moment of the attack had been imprisoned in what might well be their tomb. Holbrook Davis was there and Bill Hamel, Jim Gudbrandsen, Larry Costa, and Norman Mayer.

I spoke to them on the phone. "Fellows, this is the chaplain. You're in a tough spot, but the captain says he'll get you out, and that means just that; he'll get you out. But we can't do it yet; we can't get at you yet. The fires are being pushed back, though, so keep your chins up. You have battle lights down there? Then you're better off than we are. Play acey deucey and pray."

Many hours would elapse before the captain could keep his promise, but in the end he kept it.

The fires on the flight and gallery decks were being pushed back slowly (oh, so slowly), but pushed back far enough to let us see that still further back were six of our own thousand-pound bombs which for some reason had not yet exploded, despite the fact that they were ready armed, and had been enveloped in flames for hours. A hose crew fought through the smoke and flame toward the bombs, while another crew wet down this forward hose and the crew which manned it. They pushed to within eight feet of the bombs and then, choked with smoke, singed with flame, they set about wetting them down. Care had to be taken not to hit the bombs directly; the hose pressure would detonate the fuses. I told the boys to bounce the water on the deck and spray the bombs. The leader of the gang with characteristically American, deliciously cynical humor, turned and said, "That's right, Father; let's not take unnecessary chances!"

While the boys were spraying the bombs and Lieutenant Commander George Stone was defusing them, we were attacked by yet another Jap plane—this time a fighter. He came in fast and low, strafing the deck. All hands sprawled, crouching beneath their helmets. Placito Abellon, a Filipino boy, Chief Cook, flopped down beside me.

To him this strafing was the last straw. I've never seen, nor expect to see, a person more completely frightened. With bullets splattering around us, I said the Act of Contrition into his ear. He tried to repeat the familiar prayer, but his jaw muscles wouldn't function. He was inarticulate. I gave him absolution. Quicker than it takes to tell, the strafing was over, and we were still alive. But there was no time to rejoice. Seconds were valuable; we couldn't afford to let the flames reach those bombs again.

"Come on. We have to get back to the hoses."

Physically and psychologically unnerved, green with fright, Abbelon came back. And because it was so obvious that he had great fear to conquer, and had conquered it, his example led thirty other boys back within a matter of seconds. A good share of the credit for preventing the explosion of those six bombs must go to Abbelon.

The jettisoning of these bombs marked one of the turning points in the fight to save the ship. No more explosions occurred, except that of the small fifty-caliber bullets, belts of which had been strewn about by earlier explosions. On catching fire they would pop off like bundles of firecrackers.

The ship was no longer drifting toward Japan. We were at last under tow by the *Pittsburgh*. Joe Taylor had accomplished the almost impossible feat of seamanship called for by the captain's order, "Get the ship under tow." We were headed in the general direction of home, fully conscious, however, of the disparity of distances: Japanese shores forty miles, home shores eleven thousand miles.

The fires still threatened, but we were steadily getting them under control. Jap planes still threatened, but for the past two hours none had succeeded in breaking through the ack-ack of our guard ships.

Sunset brought a reasonable facsimile of peace, and a great increase in confidence. Earlier in the day not many would have gambled on our chances. But now, if the Jap planes didn't get in during the night, if the fires were put under control, if the gasoline continued to spew out of the main tank harmlessly, without the flames catching it; if all these "ifs" were fulfilled, we would survive. Darkness fell, and the skipper breathed easier. Of course, we were still a blazing hulk, visible for miles on the open sea, a perfect target for a night air attack; still, compared to what we had gone through already, we were comparatively well off.

According to wartime regulations, at sundown all lights must be darkened; not even a cigarette may glow on a weather deck. Just then, with a great puff of relief, Captain Gehres lit a cigarette on the bridge of his flaming ship. But he had only one puff.

"Begging the captain's pardon, sir, it's darkened ship. No cigarette on the weather deck."

Yes, it was Klimkiewicz, the captain's orderly-gunner, on duty at the mount just above the bridge.

CHAPTER EIGHT

A Ship That Will Not Die

S UNSET TIME is dinnertime, so we on the *Franklin* had our dinner. One half slice of bread (remember that bag of bread we borrowed from the *Santa Fe*) and a little bacon fat. We swallowed it with dry throats. We had no water to wash it down; we wouldn't have water for days. I ate my ration on the bridge, chatting with Captain Gehres, Commander Joe Taylor, and Commander Jurika. "Best damn' meal I ever tasted," said Joe. Relatively speaking, I guess it was.

During our supper session we talked of the events of the day. We didn't yet completely realize the proportions of the job that had been done, but we were beginning to realize. Already feats of extraordinary heroism were the talk of the ship: the spectacular rescue by Don Gary of the three hundred men trapped below, the masterful way Doc Fuelling had prevented panic among the trapped boys, the fire fighting of Graham and Morgan and Harris. Among them all, perhaps the work of Joe Taylor stood out most prominently because it seemed not so much spectacular as impossible.

"Joe, how did you get us under tow?"

"Well, Captain, when you told me to make the preparations, I just didn't know what to do, and there wasn't any chance to look it up in a book. We dropped the starboard anchor so that later we could use the chain. We improvised, and somehow we got that messenger towline across. I don't know how the boys did it, but I'd say the stewards' mates deserve an awful lot of credit. You should have heard that chant, Captain!"

Commander Bill Hale was there, too, during the brief respite. He added his tales of heroism to the saga. He told them simply, undramatically, because in most of them he had participated.

It was a pleasant sensation to be sailing along at six knots under tow by the *Pittsburgh*. Ordinarily such speed would be scorned even by a tramp steamer, let alone one of the flagships of the fast Carrier Task Force 58. But things today were not ordinary, and there is an infinite difference between being dead in the water and sailing even at six knots. Reminds me of the tired academic joke: $2 \times X$ is greater than 9×0. This session was just a reprieve, however. There was still much to be done; so we broke up and went back to work.

During the past two hours Tom Greene, the engineering officer, had been sending messengers or going himself from the fo'c'sle to the vicinity of the engine rooms, testing whether they were accessible. It was like Noah sending his doves from the ark. And just as the doves eventually found a hilltop, so in time Greene found his way into the engine room. The heat was almost unbearable, and the smoke still thick. Now the rescue breathers which had been borrowed from the *Santa Fe* came into use. Several engineering officers went down, opening what air vents they could, finding more rescue breathers, and proving by their own reactions that though the boys might suffer from the intense heat, they could endure it.

About nine o'clock, all the engineering officers and men who had been standing by, organized and ready since noon, returned to their stations. The temperature in the firerooms and the engine rooms was still about 150°, but all night long they worked, getting the fires started, building up steam, making emergency repairs, doing the thousand things necessary to bring a dead ship back to life.

A boiler watch was formed to stand by gauges as the steam pressure built up; with nobody too sure that the boilers, strained by the explosions, wouldn't blow up in their faces. James Brumfield volunteered for this job, and James Turner, Ralph Barry, John McCaffrey, Welton Howge. Theirs was the bravest kind of bravery, for the action itself concentrated their mind on the dangers and their work offered no distraction from the constant threat of imminent death. These boys deserve abundant credit, and so does *every* officer and man in the engineering department. All night long they worked through the smoke, the heat, and the danger.

While the engineers worked, some of the rest were able to take a little nap. Most of the officers' rooms in the forward section of the ship (and they were few) had not been damaged, but nearly every compartment assigned to the men had been consumed by fire. The rooms were turned over to the boys, and while they slept, two or three to a bunk, the officers carried on the work of fire fighting. Chaplain Gatlin, now freed of his task of calming and soothing the boys as they escaped from the traps below decks, joined the hose crew. "Gats" was like that, doing his job well, and when that job was done, finding another, always quietly efficient and dependable. Several times during the night the flames flared up, and there were moments when we thought that all that had been gained throughout the day would be lost by a shifting of the wind or a new gasoline explosion.

With the *Franklin*'s fires burning brightly, making her a flaming beacon visible for miles, the Jap planes returned in force against us. Their last attack had been just before sundown, before we got under tow. Carefully the Japs had calculated our position, the wind force, the currents. They determined to a nicety what our exact location would be at midnight. Directly to that spot their planes flew, ignoring the blaze some twenty miles away from their calculated objective.

Just up above the horizon a mighty air battle was now in progress—Jap fighters and bombers against fighters of Task Force 58 assigned to give us air protection. We watched the spectacle from the *Franklin*. A blinding glare in the sky, a hurtling mass of flame splashing into the sea . . . a Jap plane or one of ours? We could not tell. We didn't have a scorecard with names and numbers of all the players. Like Francis Scott Key, as he watched by night the rockets of 1814, we were in no position to know the outcome. We did not know until the flaming splashes ceased. Since no plane molested us, we gathered that most of the "splashes" were Japs. Our own fighters were flying in a great circle. Later we learned that forty Jap planes had been destroyed.

Why didn't the Japs veer from their course and direct their attack against the *Franklin?* Perhaps because they were Japanese. American pilots would immediately have recognized that their careful calculations had become useless, and would have brought a little individual initiative into play.

When the signals call for a right-end sweep and something has obviously gone wrong with the play and the whole opposing eleven is swarming in, an American boy will try to slide off left tackle. Apparently the Japs hadn't learned football. When they last observed the *Franklin*, she had been dead in the water, drifting at a definite rate in a definite direction. They refused to heed even the possibility that the situation might have changed, despite the evidence of their senses and our flaming ship. Perhaps, though, the Japs were giving an indirect tribute to the work done by Joe Taylor; they probably thought a blazing hulk the size of the *Franklin* could not possibly get a towline rigged.

All through the night planes circled the sky. Occasionally in the night breezes, a lull would waft the sound of engines to our ears, but they never came too close. They were there to protect us, not to scare us. In darkness friend and enemy cannot be distinguished; friends kept their distance and made the enemy keep theirs.

After the big air battle, and when our fires were well under control, Captain Gehres, who had not once forgotten his promise to the boys trapped in steering aft, now set about to fulfill that promise. The combat phone was still in commission. It was a mighty thrill for those on the bridge to hear the captain talking to Davis and his crew. "Lieutenant Wassman is organizing a rescue party; on the way down now; will continue to keep you informed." It was a mightier thrill to those boys on the receiving end who for seventeen hours had been trapped below. Ed Wassman and his volunteer rescue crew went aft along the flight deck, skirting the many gaping holes.

On the port side it was impossible to find a ladder, for that whole section of the ship had been blown away. On the starboard side, the ladders were twisted, but descent was possible. They passed a tired hose crew, washing away the gasoline as it still spurted along a passageway which proved to be a blind alley. They retraced their steps, winding through one passage, then another passage, but always going aft, going down. It was like exploring a jungle by dark. Old passages had been blocked off, new passages had been blown through bulkheads. A wrong turn or a false step and the rescue party might find that they themselves were trapped. Fumbling through the murk of fetid, smoke-filled compartments, clambering over and under steel debris, floundering through water at times waist high, they worked down to the compartment immediately above steering aft and found that this, too, was filled with water. Undaunted, the boys retraced their steps and returned with hand pumps.

While words of encouragement were phoned from the bridge, Davis, Gudbrandsen, and the rest could hear the new activity in the compartment above them. The level of the water was now about four feet. One of the rescuers managed to open a bulkhead door, and the pent-up water poured off into the darkness. That left only six inches sloshing about the deck, not enough to cause harm if the boys below were warned. A message was tapped to them and was answered by Davis. He swung the hatch open and the water poured down. Thus, after many anxious hours for all of us, these boys were saved.

Through these hours of the mid-watch, while the enlisted men slept in the officers' bunks, the officers continued to man the hoses, by turns catching a few winks sprawled on the deck, ready for instant emergency. Long before sunrise the ship was awake. Officers and men were tired, hungry, aware of the dangers which still beset them and of the back-breaking work ahead. But the ship was alive. The engineers had kept their promise!

We still had a half-slice of bread per man and a few more cans of bacon fat, and even a few cans of fruit juice which Lieutenant Jesse Albritton, one of the supply officers, had salvaged. Albritton had spent the night hazardously breaking into emergency storerooms. While he was still looking for emergency supplies, Frasure, the steward's mate who had composed the "Tow Chant," went with me and a half dozen of his companions to the galley storerooms in search of food. They came hesitantly, well knowing we could easily break into a compartment and find ourselves trapped there. But their very hesitation was an added tribute to their bravery. They came despite the dangers.

These Negro boys, who on the previous day had worked as courageously as any aboard, and who, by their chant, had supplied an emotional impetus which perhaps no others could have contributed, now humbly and simply returned to their routine function aboard ship, that of providing food. Our search was not particularly successful, but we found more of the now tiresome but still welcome bacon fat and fruit juice. As one of the boys said, "Our search wasn't fruitless; we brought home the bacon."

Hard work, depressing work, lay ahead. The engineers continued their task, and by nine o'clock Captain Gehres signaled the *Pittsburgh* that we could now make twelve knots on our own power. We cast off the towline. We were a living, self-sustaining ship again. But there were many hundreds aboard who were not living. Burial parties were organized in general charge of Dr. Smith. All the doctors and dentists and both chaplains, assisted by about eighty men, set about the solemn task of burying the dead.

Some bodies were easily accessible; most were not. It was like wandering through thick underbrush. Ten feet ahead you could see an object; but ten feet of entanglement lay between, and it would take fifteen minutes to break through. The decks and beams of the *Franklin* were a jungle of steel. Explosion after explosion had wrenched the ship. Rafters, "I" beams, steel mesh, steel netting, steel catwalks, steel equipment, had crashed to the decks. It was not unusual to work for a full hour, lifting, pushing, breaking through this wreckage in order to go fifteen feet to reach the body of a dead comrade. These boys had not been crushed to death; they had died in the first great flash of gasoline flame. But after death they had been enmeshed in the debris of the explosions. Our burial services were brief but they were reverent. The body of a human being is, by the grace of God, a Temple of the Holy Spirit. However brief may be the ceremony of burial at sea, there is about it something that transcends in solemnity the ceremony of any burial in a graveyard. Perhaps subconsciously the mind grasps a great and natural symbolism. As the body is consigned to the immensity of water, so the soul is consigned to the immensity of a merciful God.

All through the day the burials continued. A body would be extricated from the steel debris, gently lifted onto a stretcher, and carried to the quarterdeck. There Chaplain Gatlin or myself would say a brief prayer; and another of our former shipmates would be buried.

At one point, burials on the hangar deck were interrupted by a request made by Chief Electrician Phillips. The previous morning, at the height of the explosions, Phillips had been a leader in saving many men trapped in the main electrical compartment. He had rescued men in danger of literally roasting to death. Some he had not rescued; they were already dead. Phillips asked us now if we would bury these boys. We followed him down into the bowels of the ship, and there at the main electrical switchboard saw an example of extreme devotion to duty: four boys who had been manning the controls, dead at their stations; two others were dead on the deck beside them. With deep appreciation of the sacrifice they had made, we buried these boys who, knowing that their efforts would help to keep the ship in commission, had stayed at their posts.

Boys don't like to carry burned corpses pickaback up steep ladders. I think that I carried most of the corpses. It has been a source of several nightmares since, perhaps because on one trip I was so exhausted that I fell asleep a moment on a step of the ladder. It is disconcerting to awake and find oneself clasping and facing a burned corpse.

It was necessary to give the burial parties frequent recesses from their tiring and depressing task. It was necessary to watch them carefully lest young minds already subjected to a strain beyond that endured by most people throughout an entire lifetime might be strained to the breaking point. On one such occasion, Chaplain Gatlin came to me. "Joe, I'm just about at the end of my rope." To which I responded: "I'm glad to hear it, because I'm at the end of my rope, too. What do you think of the kids? Should we send them up to the fo'c'sle now for a rest period, or can we go on a little longer?"

A cigarette smoked in the quiet breeze of the fo'c'sle revives an American quickly. During these rest periods, I talked to the kids and they chatted among themselves. During one such recess Dr. Sam Sherman and I were talking.

"I guess Bill Fox is definitely dead. I haven't heard anything about him."

"Yes," said Sam, "he's dead. A great man. I heard how he died."

Then Sam told me what was known about the last moments of Dr. Bill Fox. When the first Jap bomb hit, Bill was in the doctor's office, third deck, on the starboard side. The explosion had left one passageway that might lead to safety. He pointed it out and directed the corpsman to get topside. "I'll go across to sick bay and see what I can do for the boys there." Shortly afterward he died there with his patients, trapped and killed by another explosion. As Sam finished his story my thoughts went back to the pre-combat Mass which Bill had served as my altar boy.

But we could not devote our complete attention to the dead while there were still boys trapped below. Time and time again the burials were interrupted as new and urgent need for rescue parties arose. About noon one boy was found badly burned, suffering from shock, and quite irrational. We should have appreciated how unstrung he was when he insisted that when we were hit he had been getting a haircut, and that another boy and the barber were still in the compartment. We should have realized that no one would be getting a haircut at seven o'clock in the morning, and during combat. But even if we had been positive that the lad was talking irrationally, we couldn't have taken a chance when a life was at stake.

So another searching party was organized. We set out for the designated compartment, sloshing through the water, bumping against debris, wondering why boys must choose the most inaccessible compartments in the ship for their informal barbershops. The place we were sent to was thoroughly searched; and no one, living or dead, was found.

While the burial parties went about their solemn task, others were detailed to clear away the wreckage. On the hangar deck and flight deck, Lieutenant Morgan and Bo'sn Frisbee were having a field day. Hundreds of tons of steel debris had to be jettisoned. No infant ever took a hammer to a clock more zestfully than these two tore apart sheets of steel. Some of the wreckage was so massive it was beyond their strength. But nothing was beyond their ingenuity. Red had a fantastic idea. In the pit of the forward elevator, four jeeps had been parked. All aboard assumed that they had been destroyed along with everything else on the hangar deck, but Red insisted on investigating. In a short time a most remarkable sight startled everyone. Four jeeps rushed about the deck dragging the heavy wreckage outboard for jettisoning.

All hands worked through the long day in searching parties, burial parties, wrecking parties, foraging parties. The supply officers used all available hands to bail out compartments, making accessible other compartments where food was known to be stored. The engineers kept at their tasks without rest and without relief. Our speed increased from twelve to fourteen to fifteen, until at night we could make sixteen knots. The electricians were repairing circuits, improvising units for the burned-out electric stoves, setting up intership communication. The radar men were even able to set up a portable radar. Lieutenant (jg) Marvin Bowman, assisted by Ed Nycum, Radar Technician 1/c, did it. How? Only those who tinker with such gadgets could ever know.

About ten o'clock at night we knocked off work. Again the boys were allowed to take over the officers' rooms and sleep. When the day's work is done it is usual for the officers to congregate in the wardroom, exchange small talk and sip coffee. We had no coffee to sip, but about ten very dry officers sat around talking. I whispered to Dr. Sherman, who had access to the medical supplies. He went out and a few minutes later came back waving a quart as though it were a banner or a trophy. Red Harris, Frisbee, and Morgan were there and a few others. They let out a cheer at the unexpected sight, "Pass that bottle!" But Red Morgan wouldn't take it from Frisbee. "Padre," he drawled, "take the bottle. Hand it to me personally. I want to be able to tell my grandchildren that aboard ship, where Navy Regs forbid it, the Padre passed me a quart of whisky and offered me a drink."

Never before had whisky been more justifiably administered for "medicinal purposes only." The liquor was quickly consumed, and then I made a speech. "Fellows, if you had been smart, you would have realized that this was just the 'come on.' You've accepted the bribe, so now you're obligated. Seriously, though, there are many more bodies that must be buried tonight. There are a dozen in the vicinity of the galley stoves. The electricians say the stoves will be ready in the morning. We must bury these bodies and clean up the galley before it will be safe to prepare food there."

That group of officers, hard, fine, tough, willing—best of the American crop—continued until the small hours of the morning at the gruesome task of burying the dead.

Wednesday was a repetition of Tuesday. The same type of work, the same lack of food, the same awareness of Jap planes about to strike. But the strain was definitely greater because of the cumulative effect of nervous tension. The engineers still worked without stop, patching and improving; the wrecking parties went on jettisoning debris. The burial parties continued burying the dead.

To force access to one of the compartments in the mangled gallery deck, Bo'sn Frisbee hacked away at a steel door which had been jammed by the explosions. Frisbee has just that laconic sort of expression that makes him seem to be chewing tobacco even when he isn't. He stopped for a moment from his arduous work. "O.K.," he said, "I'm tough and hard; I can do rough work and I think I have guts. But men like me didn't save this ship. The man up there on the bridge, he saved the ship. He's got character. He's a leader. I take my hat off to the old man."

Never has a finer tribute been paid to a commanding officer than this tribute to Captain Gehres by one of the more impassive members of his crew.

Sometime in mid-afternoon I was crossing the flight deck

with Joe Taylor to resume the burial services which I had interrupted for a special errand, when another Jap plane zoomed out of the sky and strafed us. I should have crouched to the deck to make myself as small a target as possible. I didn't crouch, but not from bravado or fearlessness. The effort involved in having to climb to my feet again seemed just then to be a greater evil than any number of bullets that might be splashing around. Perhaps one can become sated with danger. I was too tired even to be angry, and yet, subconsciously, I did resent any enemy plane strafing us while we were burying the dead.

Toward sunset that afternoon the burials were completed. The forward hangar deck had been well cleared of wreckage. The firerooms, engine rooms, machine shops, and electric switchboards were running almost normally. Word passed for all hands to muster on the forward hangar deck. An order of the day had been published on the one mimeograph machine that had survived the explosion. It was headed "A ship that won't be sunk can't be sunk." The orders read:

(1) Due to our after gasoline system being damaged smoking regulations must be strictly enforced. You may smoke on the forecastle during the daylight hours. You may smoke in the forward messing compartment between reveille and taps. Officers may smoke in the wardroom. *Never throw a lighted butt over the side.*

(2) Keep busy doing something all the time. If you aren't on a scheduled working party, work anyway. We've got the world by the tail, hang on.

(3) Do not throw *any usable article* over the side. If you think it can be salvaged, stack it neatly on the hangar deck just forward of No. 3 elevator on the starboard side.

(4) Anyone knowing the whereabouts of any musical instruments, report to the chaplain.

(5) Any personal effects such as wallets, watches, etc., shall be turned in to the Executive Officer's cabin. . . . *Signed* JOE TAYLOR, Commander, U.S. Navy, Executive Officer.

Below the official orders were written congratulatory messages. From Captain Fitz of the *Santa Fe* to Captain Gehres of the *Franklin*: "Congratulations on heroic work and outstanding efficiency of yourself and men in getting ship under way and saving her. It is an example we will never forget."

There was a message from our admiral, who had been forced to leave us to carry on operations against the Japs from another carrier. It read: "Congratulations. I may be on a stranger's doorstep now but I claim you again with pride. Battered though you may be you are still my child. Great work. *Signed*: DAVISON."

We had a hot meal that night! The ship was rapidly returning to almost normal routine. Not quite normal, however; all hands needed much sleep before they would be themselves again. And not quite routine, because all hands realized that each participated in the congratulatory messages; all hands were becoming more and more aware of a special pride in an extraordinary accomplishment. By their actions they had created a new ship's motto: "A ship that won't be sunk can't be sunk."

CHAPTER NINE

Return to the States

STEAMING JAUNTILY along at twenty-one knots, a hard-working ship, we reached Pearl Harbor on April 3rd, just one month to the day after we set out for combat.

Pearl Harbor is the big naval base of the Pacific. She underwent her own baptism of war, as all will remember. Since that first Pearl Harbor Day many a crippled warship had limped into her haven. Familiarity, even if it does not breed contempt, does definitely breed callousness. A floating wreck that would make headlines in the States could well be routine at Pearl. But somehow the *Franklin* was different.

The dispatches which had been received by Com Air Pac (Commander of Naval Air Forces in the Pacific) had everyone at Pearl Harbor waiting, wondering, looking for the docking of the *Franklin*. Then she steamed through the narrow channel past the Administration Building. She made the great turn and edged toward the pier, about to dock port side to.

When a ship enters port ceremoniously, all hands are mustered at "Quarters for entering port." On a carrier officers and men stand at attention on the flight deck. The usual complement of three thousand men at attention on the flight deck impresses most shore-side witnesses. But the *Franklin* didn't have three thousand men, and she had very little flight deck. Mustered in the forward section of the only part of the ship which was not completely battered were four hundred men (the remainder of the 706 Club were on duty at their engineering and mooring stations). In the front line port side, facing the dock, was "Saxy" Dowell's band: two horns, one accordion, two "sweet potatoes," one tire pump, one giant kettle, and two smaller kettles.

A specially organized glee club of Waves on shore began to sing as the *Franklin* edged up to the dock. They sang the traditional song of welcome, "Aloha!" Clear, feminine voices rang out loud and melodious; the *Franklin* slid closer, the girls looked; they wondered; they faltered. The song of welcome melted away. But "Saxy" sensed their embarrassment. He had to cover up their lapse. His fantastic band blared out a song which was instantly caught up by the crew.

The youngest, most sentimental Wave had nothing to be ashamed of. The eyes of that old seadog Vice Admiral George Murray were misted with tears. The only ones present who were not crying were the kids on the flight deck of the *Franklin.* They sang lustily: "Oh, the Old Big Ben, she ain't what she used to be, she ain't what she used to be, ain't what she used to be just a few days ago. Bombs in the hangar deck, Boom. Boom!"

The mooring lines were tossed. We were docked at Pearl.

This was the base at which I had been stationed until one short (or long) month ago. The week before I left to board the *Franklin,* I had sent a letter to my sister Alice in the Philippines. It is a queer sensation writing to one who may be long since dead; but on the chance that she was alive I had written to her through the Red Cross units with the Sixth Army, which had just landed in Luzon. The prisoners of Santo Tomas had been liberated, but La was not there.

Then the Japanese devastation of the old walled City of Manila began. As the daily newspapers headlined the atrocity stories, hope for La's safety waned. On the 3rd of March I boarded the *Franklin,* resigned to the fact that she was dead. Now, on the 3rd of April, the wounded but unconquered *Franklin* was back at Pearl Harbor. Amidst the bustle of activity which accompanies the mooring of a large ship, I heard a voice from the dock hailing, "Father O'Callahan."

It was Father Sheehy, district chaplain at Pearl Harbor. He had not known whether I was still alive, but he had hoped. I was soon shouting greetings to him. His greeting to me was the climax of a drama: "Hi, Joe! I can't wait until the gangway is across, I have an important appointment. I'll meet you later. I came down to tell you that yesterday we received definite word that your sister is alive in Manila!"

The voyage from Pearl Harbor to New York by way of the Panama Canal was routine, but not restful. The days were filled with work, the same hard laborious work which cleared the ship of wreckage and the mind of psychosis. The evening hours were spent in pleasant conversation. The days passed in work and talk. Of course we did a little eating once in a while, and incidentally the meals were what civilians dreamed about but did not see any more. The ship had been stocked to provide 3,400 men for four months, and the 706 Club ate well. And always we were getting closer to New York. Expectation mounted as the distance decreased. Finally the long anticipated day arrived.

As we steamed into New York harbor with all hands, in clean dungarees, once more mustered on the flight deck at "Quarters for entering port," the photographers caught a deeply symbolic picture. It typified the spirit of the men of the *Franklin*—the spirit of the men of America. Framed by a massive "I" beam which had been bent by explosions to an inverted "V," they snapped the Statue of Liberty. That was a very welcome "welcome" to New York. But there was no fanfare; because wartime security forbade publicity the *Franklin* slipped up the East River almost unnoticed.

Shortly after our unheralded arrival at the Brooklyn Navy Yard, there was a historic ceremony on the forward flight deck. Washington had checked the records of *Franklin* personnel and had assigned its experts in nuance and paraphrase to compose citations. One bright spring morning, we stood "at attention," then "at ease" on the forward flight deck. Many distinguished guests were present; but the most distinguished were the near relatives of the crew. A historic ceremony for a historic ship: A "ship that would not die" witnessed the presentation of the greatest number of decorations ever to be awarded to one ship in the history of the Navy.

The Navy Cross to Captain Gehres and to Commander Taylor. For Les, this citation:

For distinguishing himself by extraordinary heroism in operations against the enemy while serving as Commanding Officer of an aircraft carrier on 19 March 1945 when his ship was struck by enemy bombs which caused tremendous fires and explosions among a large number of fully armed and fueled planes both on the flight deck and in the hangar. Although handicapped by severe damage to his ship's fire-fighting equipment and communications system, he displayed outstanding resourcefulness in directing the measures which eventually brought the fires under control, got power back to his ship, and enabled her to be withdrawn from a position close aboard a hostile coast. His skill and courage were at all times in keeping with the highest traditions of the United States Naval Service.

As I listened to the citation for Joe Taylor, my memory relived the scene on the fo'c'sle:

Gold Star in lieu of the third Navy Cross:

For distinguishing himself by extraordinary heroism in operations against the enemy while serving as Executive Officer of an aircraft carrier which was striking the Japanese home islands in the vicinity of Kobe, Japan, on 19 March 1945. When his ship was hit and severely damaged by enemy air attacks and rocked by violent explosions of her own ordnance, he supervised and directed the efforts to save the ship, controlling raging fires, flooding magazines and personally leading and participating in the jettisoning of heated live ammunition and bombs. With utmost disregard for his personal safety, he visited all sections of the badly damaged ship, leading, inspiring the crew in the gallant and successful effort to salvage the drifting and erupting carrier. In the face of further enemy attacks and explosions of the carrier's own arms he took charge of the towing operations which resulted in getting his ship underway. His cool, calm determination and outstanding leadership were an inspiration to all officers and men, and contributed greatly to the ultimate saving of the ship. His conduct throughout was in keeping with the highest traditions of the United States Naval Service.

Two awards were not presented on the *Franklin* that day. A short time later President Truman conferred the Congressional Medal of Honor upon Lieutenant Gary and upon Father O'Callahan, S.J. Citation for the Congressional Medal of Honor was conferred upon Lieutenant Donald A. Gary, U.S.N.:

For conspicuous gallantry and intrepidity at the risk of his life above and beyond the call of duty as an Engineering Officer attached to the U.S.S. *Franklin* when that vessel was fiercely attacked by enemy aircraft during operations against the Japanese Home Islands near Kobe, Japan, 19 March 1945. Stationed on the third deck when the ship was rocked by a series of violent explosions . . . Lieutenant Gary unhesitatingly risked his life to assist several hundred men trapped in a messing compartment filled with smoke, and with no apparent egress. As the imperiled men below decks became increasingly panic-stricken under the raging fury of incessant explosions, he confidently assured them he would find a means of effecting their release and, groping through the dark, debris-filled corridors, ultimately discovered an escapeway. Staunchly determined, he struggled back to the messing compartment three times despite menacing flames, flooding water and the ominous threat of sudden additional explosions, on each occasion calmly leading his men through the blanketing pall of smoke until the last one had been saved. Selfless in his concern for his ship and his fellows, he constantly rallied others about him, repeatedly organized and led fire-fighting parties into the blazing inferno on the flight deck and, when fire-rooms 1 and 2 were found to be inoperable, entered the No. 3 fireroom and directed the raising of steam in one boiler in the face of extreme difficulty and hazard. An inspiring and courageous leader, Lieutenant Gary rendered self-sacrificing service under the most perilous conditions and, by his heroic initiative, fortitude and valor, was responsible for the saving of several hundred lives. His conduct throughout reflects the highest credit upon himself and upon the United States Naval Service.

Citation for Father Joseph T. O'Callahan, S.J.:

For conspicuous gallantry and intrepidity at the risk of his life above and beyond the call of duty while serving as Chaplain on board the U.S.S. *Franklin* when that vessel was fiercely attacked by enemy Japanese aircraft during offensive operations near Kobe, Japan, on 19 March 1945. A valiant and forceful leader, calmly braving the perilous barriers of flame and twisted metal to aid his men and his ship, Lieutenant Commander O'Callahan groped his way through smoke-filled corridors to the flight deck and into the midst of violently exploding bombs, shells, rockets and other armament. With the ship rocked by incessant explosions, with debris and fragments raining down and fires raging in ever increasing fury, he ministered to the wounded and dying, comforting and encouraging men of all faiths; he organized and led fire-fighting crews into the blazing inferno on the flight deck; he directed the jettisoning of live ammunition and the flooding of the magazine; he manned a hose to cool hot, armed bombs rolling dangerously on the listing deck, continuing his efforts despite searing, suffocating smoke which forced men to fall back gasping and imperiled others who replaced them. Serving with courage, fortitude and deep spiritual strength, Lieutenant Commander O'Callahan inspired the gallant officers and men of the *Franklin* to fight heroically and with profound faith in the face of almost certain death and return their stricken ship to port.

But we were talking about a historic ceremony aboard a historic ship. On this day in the Brooklyn Navy Yard, many more Navy Crosses were presented, and with each presentation, a citation of unique and special bravery. Navy Crosses to Commanders Hale, Smith, Jurika. (At Hawaii, Steve had heard that his mother in the Philippines had been killed by the Japs, about the time I had heard that my sister had been spared.) A Navy Cross for Dr. Fox, my altar boy at "The Last Mass," was awarded posthumously.

Navy Crosses went to Greene, McKinney, Kreamer, Downes, Stone, and to Mac Kilpatrick, whose worth I had come to appreciate at the time of the transfer of the stretcher cases to the *Santa Fe*. To Sam Sherman and Jim Fuelling and Bill Ellis were awarded Navy Crosses for heroism beyond the call of duty.

Fred (Red) Harris received a Navy Cross. I saw his lips quiver and his eyes blink back tears as he heard the citation. Navy Crosses also went to Morgan and "Slim" Hall and Gunner Stoops.

Chaplain Grimes W. Gatlin received the Silver Star. I know he deserved that and greater honors. The boys he cared for know he deserved it. I have failed thus far to tell you that "Gats," like Red Harris, comes from Texas, a state big enough to acknowledge his greatness. I hope, too, that his church recognizes the man he is.

There yet remain 22 citations for the Silver Star, 114 citations for the Bronze Star, and 234 Special Letters of Commendation. The sum total of awards was 393, for one ship, in one day's combat.

The Ceremony of Awards on the *Franklin* was so impressive that I became somewhat saddened, not for myself, but for my mother. I knew how she felt. However greatly her son might be honored at a later date in the White House, the cold fact was that when all the ship was honored, her son's name was not mentioned.

Here Captain Les Gehres reached his noble best. Unknown to me, he talked a long time to my mother. He told her his version of what I had done for the men of the *Franklin* and for the *Franklin*.

Captain Gehres is not a sentimental man; of this I approve. Nor is he a religious man; and of this I disapprove. But Captain Gehres made my mother very happy when, after recounting my exploits, he concluded: "I am not a religious man, but during the height of combat, while I watched your son, I said aloud then, as I say to you now, 'If Faith can do that for a man, there must be something in it.'"

I mention this personal tribute from my captain, not for its value as a tribute, though I admit to being proud of it, but for its accuracy as a description of what I felt that morning of disaster. God knows I am not, as a man, more courageous than others, nor did I in fact perform more deeds of courage than many others. There is no measuring rod for heroism, anyway. But what I did do was done from Faith. I was conscious of my office as a priest and conscious of the tremendous graces that continually sustained me in fulfilling that office. Whatever I did was given me to do. It was done from Faith, which is a gift.

It is a remarkable thing that Les Gehres recognized that; and perhaps for him, too, it was a beginning of Faith. I hope so.

I stood at attention on the *Franklin* and heard the log of my shipmates' extraordinary bravery recounted in the citations, and my mind's eye caught the spirit of their heroism and my memory relived their exploits.

Jim Adam on duty at one of the ship's boilers, and when that station was untenable, coming up to the flight deck to help us control somewhat different fires.

Jerry Smith. I had started to give him a lecture in ethics against silly methods of suicide at the height of combat. But he saved a valued hose line for the ship.

Now I knew the story of Ed Mesial. I had wondered what had happened to him: "Managed to crawl on my stomach to the catwalk. I lay there hoping my strength would return; our ship listed heavily to starboard and I tumbled right onto the *Santa Fe*."

The comic-tragic touch of makeshift breeches buoys made of mailbags. They were needed to get the admirals and their staff off the ship to carry on the offensive from other ships. I saw Gerry Bogan's red hair bristling at the seeming ignominy of leaving a ship in distress.

Mailbags for admirals and mattresses for Marines. Cranstrom showed twenty buddies how to dash through flames, protected only by mattresses.

Wally Klimkiewicz, the captain's orderly: "Begging the captain's pardon, sir, a Marine can do anything. Request permission to join the gun crew . . . Begging the captain's pardon, sir . . . No cigarette on the weather deck."

"That's right, Father; let's not take unnecessary chances!"

The sun was shining full in my face, and it was a long time to stand at attention. They were reading the citations for Chase, Brown, Charnstrom, Allen. . . . Letters of Commendation for Lake . . . Buja . . . Poff . . .

The sun must have been very strong in my eyes. I had to blink against it quite often.

Appendix

During the period 14 through 22 March 1945, the composition of Task Force 58 was as follows:

Vice Admiral Mitscher

58.1, Carrier Task Group One, COMCARIDIV 5, Rear Admiral Clark (58.1.1)

USS *Hornet* (CV 12)	CVG 17
USS *Wasp* (CV 18)	CVG 86
USS *Bennington* (CV 20)	CVG 82
USS *Belleau Wood* (CVL 24)	CVLG 30

58.1.2, Support Unit, COMBATDIV 8, Rear Admiral Shafroth
USS *Indiana* (BB 58)
USS *Massachusetts* (BB 59)

58.1.22, COMCRIDIV 14, Rear Admiral Whiting
USS *Vincennes* (CL 64)
USS *Vicksburg* (CL 86)
USS *Miami* (CL 89)

58.1.3, Screen, COMDESRON 61, Captain Carter, DESDIVS 61, 121, 122, 25, 49 & 50

USS *Shroeder* (DD 501)	USS *Mansfield* (DD 728)
USS *Sigspee* (DD 502)	USS *L. K. Swenson* (DD 729)
USS *Harrison* (DD 573)	USS *Collett* (DD 730)
USS *J. Rodgers* (DD 574)	USS *Maddox* (DD 731)
USS *McKee* (DD 575)	USS *Blue* (DD 744)
USS *Murray* (DD 576)	USS *Brush* (DD 745)
USS *Dashiell* (DD 659)	USS *Taussig* (DD 746)
USS *DeHaven* (DD 727)	USS *S. N. Moore* (DD 747)

58.2, Carrier Task Group Two, COMCARDIV 2, Rear Admiral
Davison (58.2.1)
USS *Franklin* (CV 13) .... CVG 5
USS *Hancock* (CV 19) .... CVG 19
USS *Bataan* (CVL 29) .... CVLG 47
USS *San Jacinto* (CVL 30) .... CVLG 45

58.2.2, Support Unit, COMCRUDIV 10, Rear Admiral Wiltse
COMBATDIV 6, Rear Admiral Cooley

58.2.21, Battleships
USS *North Carolina* (BB 55)
USS *Washington* (BB 56)

58.2.22, Cruisers
USS *Baltimore* (CA 68)
USS *Pittsburgh* (CA 72)
USS *Santa Fe* (CLAA 60)

58.2.3, Screen, COMDESRON 52, Captain Womble, DESDIVS
103, 104, 53, 105, 106

USS *Miller* (DD 535)	USS *Hancock* (DD 675)
USS *Owen* (DD 536)	USS *Marshall* (DD 676)
USS *The Sullivans* (DD 537)	USS *Stockham* (DD 683)
USS *S. Potter* (DD 538)	USS *Wedderburn* (DD 684)
USS *Tingey* (DD 539)	USS *Halsey Powell* (DD 686)
USS *Weining* (DD 540)	USS *Uhlmann* (DD 687)
USS *Colahan* (DD 658)	USS *Benham* (DD 796)
USS *Hickox* (DD 673)	USS *Cushing* (DD 979)
USS *Hunt* (DD 674)	

58.3, Carrier Task Group Three, COMCARDIV 1, Rear Admiral
Sherman (58.3.1)
USS *Essex* (CV 9) .... CVG 83
USS *Bunker Hill* .... CVG 84
USS *Cabot* (CVL 28) .... CVLG 29

58.3.2, Heavy Support, COMBATRON 2, Vice Admiral Lee
USS *South Dakota* (BB 57)
USS *New Jersey* (BB 62)

58.3.3, Light Support, COMCRUDIV 17, Rear Admiral Jones
USS *Pasadena* (CL 65)
USS *Springfield* (CL 66)
USS *Astoria* (CL 90) on March 19 sent to 58.2
USS *Indianapolis* (CA 35)
USS *Wilkes-Barre* (CL 103)

58.3.4, Screen, COMDESRON 62, Captain Higgins,
    COMDESDIVS 123, 124, 48, 95, 96

USS *Walker* (DD 517)	USS *Sperry* (DD 697)
USS *Erben* (DD 631)	USS *Ault* (DD 698)
USS *Hale* (DD 642)	USS *Waldron* (DD 699)
USS *Stembel* (DD 644)	USS *Haynsworth* (DD 700)
USS *Bullard* (DD 660)	USS *Weeks* (DD 701)
USS *Kidd* (DD 661)	USS *Hank* (DD 702)
USS *Black* (DD 666)	USS *Lind* (DD 703)
USS *Chauncey* (DD 667)	USS *Borie* (DD 704)
USS *English* (DD 696)	

58.4, Carrier Task Group Four, COMCARDIV 6, Rear Admiral
    Radford (58.4.1)
USS *Enterprise* (CV 6) .... CV(N)G 90
USS *Yorktown* (CV 10) .... CVG 9
USS *Intrepid* (CV 11) .... CVG 10
USS *Independence* .... CVLG 46
USS *Langley* (CVL 27) .... CVLG 23

58.4.2, Support Unit, COMCRUDIV 16, Rear Admiral Low

58.4.21, COMBATDIV 9, Rear Admiral Hanson, Battleship Sup-
    port
USS *Missouri* (BB 63)
USS *Wisconsin* (BB 64)

58.4.22, Cruiser Support
USS *Alaska* (CB 1) joined 58.2 on 19 March
USS *Guam* (CB 2) joined 58.2 on 19 March
USS *Saint Louis* (CL 49)
USS *San Diego* (CLAA 53)
USS *Flint* (CLAA 97) joined 58.2 on 19 March

58.4.3, Screen, COMDESRON 47, Captain Nunn, COMDESDIVS 93, 94, 54, 107, 108

USS *Trathen* (DD 530)
USS *Hazelwood* (DD 531)
USS *Heerman* (DD 532)
USS *McCord* (DD 534)
USS *Franks* (DD 554)
USS *Haggard* (DD 555)
USS *Hailey* (DD 556)
USS *McGowan* (DD 678)
USS *McNair* (DD 679)

USS *Melvin* (DD 680)
USS *Remey* (DD 688) joined 58.2 on 19 March
USS *N. Scott* (DD 690) joined 58.2 on 19 March
USS *Mertz* (DD 691) joined 58.2 on 19 March
USS *Monssen* (DD 798) joined 58.2 on 19 March

Navy Department

Bureau of Naval Personnel
WASHINGTON 25, D.C.

Memorandum

Subject: Awards given to personnel aboard the U.S.S. *Franklin* for action on 19 March 1945.

1. Records of the Bureau indicate the below listed men have been awarded decorations for action on 19 March 1945 while attached to the U.S.S. *Franklin*.

Medal of Honor
LCDR. Joseph Timothy O'CALLAHAN
Lt. (jg) Donald A. GARY

Navy Cross
Capt. Leslie E. GEHRES
CDR. Henry H. HALE
CDR. Joseph TAYLOR
CDR. Stephen JURIKA
CDR. Francis K. SMITH
LCDR. George William Fox (MC)(Post)
LCDR. Thomas J. GREENE
LCDR. William R. McKINNEY
LCDR. Walter H. KREAMER
LCDR. Robert B. DOWNES
LCDR. George STONE
LCDR. Mac G. KILPATRICK
LCDR. Sam SHERMAN (MC)
LCDR. James J. FUELLING
Lt. William S. ELLIS
Lt. Fred HARRIS
Lt. (jg) Lindsey E. MORGAN

Ens. Fred M. HALL
Gunner Thomas M. STOOPS

Silver Star Medal
LCDR. David BERGER
Lt. Grimes W. GATLIN
Lt. Ernest B. RODGERS
Lt. (jg) Joseph B. TIARA
Lt. (jg) Bill J. WHITE
Lt. (jg) Stanley S. GRAHAM
Lt. (jg) Edward H. R. WASSMAN
1st Lt. Walter M. NEWLAND
Ens. Robert D. McCRARY
Ch. Mach. Clarence B. REID
Mach. Walter E. MACOMBER
Boatswain Marion FRISBEE
Mach. William E. GREEN
Air. Tech. Donald H. RUSSELL
HAMEL, William H., EM3
MILLER, Charles E., SF1
STONE, Harold S., RT1
GUDBRANDSEN, James H., MM1
ABBOTT, Gilbert P., QM3
DAVIS, Holbrook R., QM3
COSTA, Laurentino "E.", MM3
MAYER, Norman C., S1

Gold Star in lieu of Second Bronze Star Medal
Lt. Melvin M. TAPPEN
Lt. (jg) Gordon L. HASSIG
Lt. (jg) Robert M. THAYER
Ch. Electrician Elmer C. PHILLIPS
Ch. Carpenter Lewis R. EDDINS

Bronze Star Medal
LCDR. John D. WHITAKER
LCDR. Lewis F. DAVIS
LCDR. DeVon M. HZER
LCDR. James W. WEST, Jr.

LCDR. Herbert A. Magnuson
Major John Stack
Major Herbert T. Elliott, Jr.
Lt. Bart Slattery
Lt. Charles G. Durr
Lt. Clyde H. Fellows, Jr.
Lt. Elmer L. Fox
Lt. James A. Vaughn, Jr.
Lt. Frank C. Cheney
Lt. Charles Carr
Lt. George W. Cheney, Jr.
Lt. Philip O. Geir, Jr.
Lt. John B. Barr
Lt. Edward Monsour
Lt. Charles B. Turek
Lt. Robert H. Frank
Lt. Jesse M. Albritton, Jr.
Lt. Theodore T. Huntington
Lt. Frederick S. Robertson, Jr.
Lt. George R. Watkins
Lt. (jg) John P. Ryder
Lt. (jg) Robert J. Wineman
Lt. (jg) Joe Aizpuru
Lt. (jg) Everett J. Taylor
Lt. (jg) Maurice M. Brundige
Lt. (jg) William K. Helzel
Lt. (jg) George B. Ritz
Lt. (jg) John B. O'Donnell
Lt. (jg) Marvin Leff
Lt. (jg) Hugh W. Close, Jr.
Lt. (jg) Marvin K. Bowman
Lt. (jg) Donald R. E. Barnaby
Lt. (jg) Walter Nardelli
1st Lt. John Skorich
Ens. Guy S. Marshall
Ens. William A. McClellan
Ens. Frederick S. Lightfoot
Ens. Richard E. Jortberg

Ens. C. PROBST
Ens. George A. HAMILTON
Ch. Gunner Walter S. HATCHER
Ch. Torpedoman John M. KALVIN
Ch. Pay Clerk Alvin L. FOWLER
Ch. Pay Clerk John W. SHEPARD, Jr.
Gunner Roy G. HALE
Acting Pay Clerk Harold LEBLANC
BROWN, John Franklin, Y2 (T)(Post)
DURRANCE, Benjamin Myron, CSF (AA)(Post)
VALLONI, Thomas J., CEM
ORENDORFF, Carl S., ACOM
MACALLISTER, William H., EM1
MCCAFFREY, John W., WT1
BRUMFIELD, James I., WT1
TURNER, James W., WT1
BARRY, Ralph (n), WT1
ABELLON, Placito, CCK
ODOM, James P., MM1
LOCKE, Robert (n), Jr., SF1
MONKUS, Frank (n), SF1
NOBLE, Charles M., BM1
FOWLER, William J., Jr., AOM1
NYCUM, Edward C., RT1
KIDWELL, Irving L., Y2
HOLSTROM, Edward (n), MM2
NOTT, William J., MM2
WELLMAN, Frederick E., MM2
FRIEDMAN, Herman S., SF2
TAMMEAID, Niloai, BM2
RYAN, Virgil R., QM2
GOWEN, Michael (n), GM2
DICKSON, Robert C., S/Sgt.
WILLIAMS, Wilfred "J.", Y3
STREICH, Hans A., WT3
CHAMBERS, Patrick A., WT3
LINDBERG, John H., EM2
FINKENSTEDT, Charles L., SSML3

BOWMAN, Alex E., Y3
BROWNING, William L., SM3
HART, Stephen C., SM3
OXLEY, Robert W., GM3
CARTWRIGHT, John E., GM3
REYNOLDS, William W., AerM3
ALEMIDA, Arthur S., AOM3
KISSELL, Lynn M., AOM2
ASTORIAN, Gerald E., S1
JACOBS, Charles W., S1
BOYD, Robert L., S1
GUGLIELMO, William (n), S1
WILSON, Dorris W., S1
OLIVER, Audrey L., S1
ALBRECHT, William R., S2
MOZDIAK, Henry J., S2
RICKS, Benjamin M., S1
TUCKER, Charles V., S1
HOTTINGER, Eugene J., S1
HOPKINS, Joseph P., S1
KLEIBER, Bernard (n), WT2
COLLINS, Arthur L., F1
HOGGE, Wilton G., F1 (WT)
SMITH, John F., F1
LA BLANCO, Joseph (n), S2
KLIMKIEWICZ, Wallace L., Pvt.
CHASE, Frank T., Jr., S2
BROWN, Paul W., S2
CHARNSTROM, Lloyd E., Pfc.
ALLEN, Edward T., Pfc.

Letters of Commendation (Ribbon)
LAKE, James (n), GM3
DUDIAK, Peter Paul, S1
CROWTHER, Thomas Dwight, GM2
FULLER, Billie (n), BM1
BUJA, John Michael, GM3
CESAR, John Norman, GM3

DE ROCHE, Edward Thomas, GM3
POFF, Calvin Robert, S2
WISE, Charles Paul, S2
BRUNN, Wilby Francis, S2
STEINBRON, Harold Ray, FCO3
CHRISTMAN, Frederick William, S2 (GM)
DARRINGTON, Keith Olsen, S1
BURKE, Russell Emmett, S1
SWANN, Bert (n), BM2
JACKSON, Dan (n), CK1
BROWN, Charles (n), CK1
SHAW, Dudley Emanuel, StM2
BAKER, William Latta, CMM
LECUS, Edward (n), MM1
BERESKA, Paul (n), MM1
MEGGINS, Charles Curtis, MM1
SLIFIES, Robert Ulysses, MM2
LEPORE, Frank Peter, MM3
GOBRIGALL, Calvin Frank, MM3
RAY, Gerald Abniwake, F2
BOLOPUE, Herman Carl, F1
SOLTVEDT, John Phillip, MM1
STITES, John Talbert, GMM
SKEAN, William (n), MM2
RAMEY, Glenn Thomas, MMR2
O'NEILL, Ernest Frank, F1
CHASSE, Richard Damasse, F1
LONG, Henry Arthur, MM3
DEFILLIPO, Michael Vincent, MoMM3
CURTIS, Thomas Franklin, MMS2
GASSMAN, Robert Francis, F1
KIELISZAK, Raymond John, F1
LAZERSKI, Richard Joseph, S1
PETERMAN, John Allen, FC2
CUSICK, James J.
O'CONNELL, Richard Daniel, S1
MANTONE, Antonio, S1
OXLEY, Robert William, GM3

CALDWELL, Charles Guy, BM1
DOWELL, Horace Kirby, Mus1
KINCAIDE, Robert Doane, Mus2
WATSON, James Kenneth, Mus2
BERGMAN, Earl Allen, Mus2
O'DONOVAN, John Richard, QM2
TARR, Bernard (n), Jr., S2
VARILEN, William (n), QM1
WALSH, Eugene Thomas, QM3
RUSSELL, Allen Clarence, S1
DAY, Robert Wayne, S2
ANDERSON, Willie "B," StM2
BROOKS, Floyd (n), StM2
LITTLE, Major (n), StM1
MATTHEWS, William R., StM2c
GLOSSOM, Sylvester (n), StM1
BARTLEY, Albert (n), StM2
DICKERSON, Leslie J., StM1
PEARSON, Ernest (n), StM2
COBB, James (n), StM2
GRIER, Edward A., StM2
GIBSON, Howard (n), StM2
GORDON, Arnold E., Ck2
RHODES, Robert Tiennie, StM2
WILLIAMS, Mack Henry, StM1
ABAGON, Angel (n), CST(AA)
GREGORY, William Tency, StM1
BROWN, Don Graviel, StM2
CULBERSON, Leonz (n), StM2
DENNIS, Jeff (n), StM2
COFFIE, Thomas (n), StM2
FRANCIS, Edward (n), StM2
GRANT, Eugene Newton, StM2
MARKS, Leon (n), StM2
BOULTON, Ulysses (n), StM2
BASHAM, John Russell, RM3
KUSY, John Michael, Prtr3
LAWSON, David Vernon, S1

BOYCE, Joseph Walton, S1
RAUSCH, Harold Edwin, S2
MCGOUGH, William Joseph, Y3
COX, John James, RM3
MILLER, George Edward, S1
PETRILL, Frank Gilbert, S2
ANTALL, Richard Charles, S1
Ens. Norman Arthur EICHNER
MIHAL, Victor Michael, RM3
RITCHIE, Edward Augusta, S1
KASSOVER, Martin Lewis, SM3
PRATHER, Donald Eugene, AMM1
JONES, James Leonard, EM3
CALDWELL, William Bowles, EM3
STORK, Glenn Dean, F1
ZELLER, Heinz (n), S2
SPRIGGS, Robert Lee, EM2
RICHARDSON, Haron James, CEM
DYER, Joseph Arthur, F1
ELSEY, Gordon John, EM1
FREGGENS, Robert Alfred, F1
DUNN, Charles Rex, EM2
SUTHERLAND, Hiram Daniel, EM3
CLINGERMAN, Kermit Gene, S1
HOPKINS, Leo Francis, RM3
PRIVETT, William Allen, MM1
MATSON, Ernest (n), SM2
MUNZING, Harry Ernest, S1
ROBINSON, John Wallace, S2
DODARO, Louis (n), RM3
DROLSOM, James Hilo, S1
COOK, Ralph Marcello, ART1
WOOK, Chester Roy, S1
BURTON, Edward Arthur, S2
BURTON, Vernon Luke, RM2
GRESHKO, Stephen (n), S1
MARTIN, Voley Arval, S2
ELLIS, Thomas Ollie, S2
PEDERSON, Harry LeRoy, S1

BLANCO, John Eliss, Jr., BM2
RAFUSE, John Oscar, GM3
GEHELNIK, Dave George, S2
LANGLEY, John Steward, S2
CATT, Harold Raymond, S2
COLE, Russell Edgar, S2
CULLEN, Charles Albert, S2
WILLARD, Henry Kellogg, II, S2
CODY, Charles Lewis, S2
GATULIS, Joseph William, GM2
WILLS, Scott William, Cox
DROUIN, Leo Willie, WT3
ROY, Henry Napoleon, F2
ROOT, Gordon Harvey, F2
HAMM, Robert Lee, WT3
DUNNE, James Louis, WT3
Lt. (jg) George Kensley LEITCH
BRENNER, William Ernest, WT3
WOLLETT, Clair "C," WT3
BIRCH, George Bobby, WT1
NICHELSON, Jack Alexander, WT1
STEWART, Robert Charles, CB
SWANSON, Robert Walter, WT2
MURPHY, Rex Gluck, B3
STRATTON, John Ross, F1
VAUGHN, William Thomas, AMM2
LARSEN, Stephen Lorang, S2
MOLLETT, Samuel Wesley, S1
FRIEND, Alon Louis, S2
HANDROP, Jack Corbet, S1
HANNA, Isom (n), S2
HAND, John Willard, AMM3
BERGIN, Kyran Francis, AMM2
THOMAS, Earl Roy, Jr., RdM1
HAMPTON, John Emmitt, AOM2
CORLISS, Wayne Albert, S1
GRAVES, Earl Eugene, AMM2
GUBA, Henry Arthur, Jr., S1
SHERWOOD, John (n), S1

LITTLEFIELD, Dewey Carl, S2
JACOBS, Harold Wilbury, S1
MARQUESS, Lawrence Calvert, S1
LUDLOW, Myron Edward, S1
SNYDER, Harold Thomas, S2
BONINE, Donald Leander, S2
FINNEY, Charles Fenton, Jr., S1
GLASBERG, Irving (n), S1
Lt. Harry Woods ARTZ
Lt. John Vincent HEDDELL
Ch. Electrician Arthur Hinsen HOFFNER
Ch. Electrician Joseph Jacobs WOLFE
Ch. Machinist Edwin August SCHWENKNER
Mach. Albert Louis HEAD
Mach. George EDE, Jr.
Ens. Clyde "T" MASSEY
Ens. Rudolph Ernest SCHMALZ
Ens. William Birch HAYLOR
Lt. (jg) Robert Thomas CONNOLLY
Mach. Allen Garfield ENSIGN
Ens. John Reilly TUCKER, Jr.
THOMAS, Harold Leslie, F1
YEARICK, Robert Day, F1
ANDREWS, Robert Frederick, EM1
DYICKANOWSKI, Andrew (n), MM2
Lt. (jg) Kenneth Paul ROCKHILL
CROFF, Donald Eugene, F1
WAYMAN, Ronan Edward, MM1
COLE, Frederick Thomas, F2
KNOELLER, William Warren, WT3
BARNES, Franklyn Ralph, MM3
KRAUSE, Leonard Robert, F2
LA ROLE, Arthur Dorsey, F1
HUTTON, Stanley Richard, F2
DRESSEL, William Richard, F1
LUPTAK, Louis William, F1
FREEK, George Marshall, Jr., F2
FRANDLE, Gerald Truman, F2

COLLUM, James Harold, F2
HARRIS, James Samuel, F2
LONG, James Moore, WT3
GILES, Raymond Gerald, WT3
McRAE, Donald Elliott, WT2
LEIPEL, Clayton Buford, WT3
PERSONEN, Veikko William, WT3
HARRIS, James Houston, F2
FURROW, John Harry, F2
WEBSTER, Hubert Cread, F2
BRYANT, Mathew William, F2
ADELSON, Albert (n), WT3
HALL, Stanley David, WT1
WHITE, John Montague, WT2
PETRUNYAK, Emery Louis, F1
OXFORD, John Marvin, F2
ROACH, John Marvin, F2
BLACKWELL, Ralph (n), F2
HALL, Leonard Melford, WT2
MAGEE, Paul Leland, MM1
ELLIS, Leon Stanley, MM1
RICCHETTI, Paul Anthony, MM2
Moses, Benjamin (n), WT2
SIEBOLD, Donald Alfred, WT3
WEINLEY, Harold DeWayne, F1
ST. PETERS, Robert Edward, EM3
Lt. Peter T. MASON (HC)
Lt. Ross E. WALES
Lt. (jg) Harold W. RICHARDSON
Ens. Harrison D. MITCHELL
SEVERSON, Royal Roscoe, SK1
Lt. Melvern C. WOOKBURN
Lt. Donald J. FITZGERALD
Lt. William McGUIRE
Lt. Donald G. BILLINGTON
Lt. Joseph F. McMEEL
RIZZI, Vito (n), SK1